ALBERTO MORROCCO

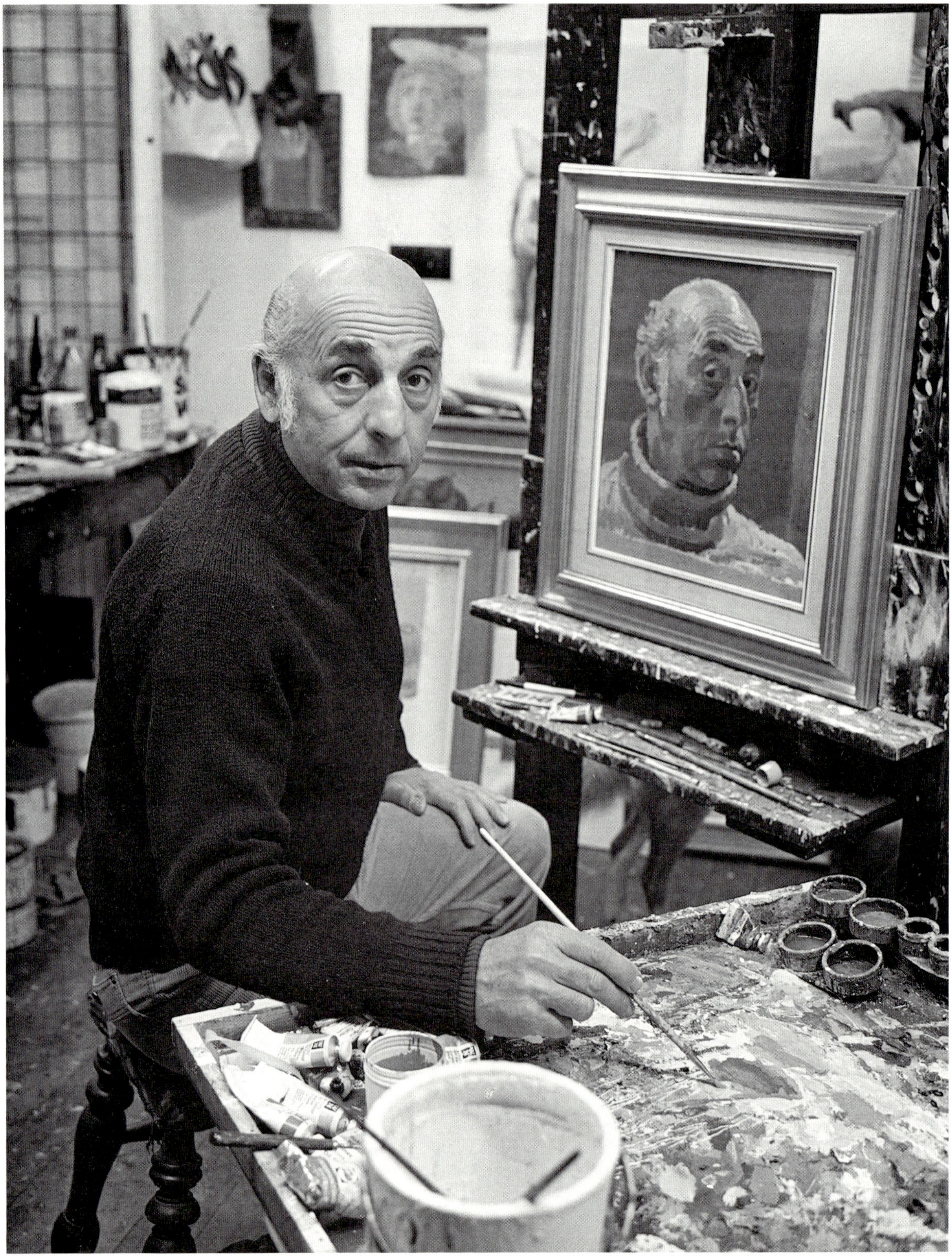

Alberto Morrocco in his Studio (Photo by Alex Coupar, ABIIP, AMPA)

Morrocco

ALBERTO MORROCCO

VICTORIA KELLER AND CLARA YOUNG

MAINSTREAM
PUBLISHING

EDINBURGH AND LONDON

PHOTOGRAPHIC CREDITS

Alex Coupar, ABIIP AMPA: Frontispiece, Plates 87, 88 and 90
Dundee Art Galleries and Museums: Plates 1 and 22
Aberdeen Art Gallery and Museums: Plates 13 and 46
Hunterian Art Gallery, University of Glasgow: Plate 48
Talbot Rice Gallery, University of Edinburgh: Plate 65
Glasgow Art Galleries and Museums: Plate 19
The Scottish Arts Council: Plate 62
Robert Fleming Holdings Limited: Plate 70
Bill Brady: Plates 76 and 78
Unknown Photographers: Plates 9, 23, 24, 25, 29, 40 and 44
Colin Ruscoe: all other Plates

First published in Great Britain in 1993 by
MAINSTREAM PUBLISHING COMPANY (EDINBURGH) LTD
7 Albany Street, Edinburgh EH1 3UG

ISBN 1 85158 590 7 (cloth)
ISBN 1 85158 591 5 (paper)

A catalogue record for this book is available from the British Library

This publication has been sponsored by the N. S. Macfarlane Charitable Trust. It has also been supported by a donation from Robert Fleming Holdings Ltd. The Scottish Arts Council has also provided financial assistance.

Typeset in Garamond by Litho Link Ltd, Welshpool, Powys, Wales
Designed by Wide Art, Edinburgh
Printed in Great Britain by Butler & Tanner Ltd, Frome

CONTENTS

ACKNOWLEDGMENTS

This book is being published to coincide with what is amazingly Alberto Morrocco's first major career retrospective. It has long been the intention of Dundee Art Galleries and Museums to organise this exhibition as a tribute to Alberto Morrocco on the occasion of his seventy-fifth birthday. Dundee is immensely indebted to him for his outstanding contribution to the visual arts in the city through his long, colourful and dynamic leadership of the School of Painting at Duncan of Jordanstone College of Art.

While the retrospective was always something we could hope to achieve within our own resources, this illustrated book, on the other hand, has only been made possible by the very generous sponsorship of the N. S. Macfarlane Charitable Trust and a substantial and welcome donation from Robert Fleming Holdings Limited. We are most grateful to both these bodies for their invaluable support for the book.

We are also indebted to the Scottish Arts Council in two ways: firstly for making a useful financial contribution towards this publication; and secondly for invaluable support in 1992 in the way of a project development grant enabling us to employ a freelance researcher whose task it was to trace and help select examples of work by one of Scotland's most versatile and prolific artists. We are very grateful to Victoria Keller for the effective and enthusiastic way she has carried out this research.

In a project of this size – the book and the exhibition – a great many people are involved. I should like to thank most warmly all the private individuals and the staff of art galleries and other institutions who have so kindly agreed to lend their pictures for the exhibition. We are also grateful to the many other collectors who assisted us with the research by sending photographs and information or else inviting us to their homes to have a look. In tracing owners of paintings we are greatly indebted to the enthusiastic co-operation of the Royal Scottish Academy (Joanna Soden); the Scottish Gallery (Guy Peploe and Robin McClure); the Thackeray Gallery, London (Priscilla Anderson); the Loomshop Gallery, Lower Largo (James Mowat); and the Open Eye Gallery, Edinburgh (Pam and Tom Wilson).

The artist joins with me in thanking Duncan Macmillan (my old teacher) for his warm support and for writing the Foreword. Closer to home, I greatly appreciated the tremendous help given by my many District Council colleagues, especially the Art Section team. I am grateful to Anne Gallacher for transcribing the interview tapes.

The District Council gratefully acknowledges the generous financial support for the promotion of the exhibition itself received from Scottish Enterprise Tayside.

Finally, my special thanks are due to Alberto Morrocco himself and his wife, Vera. Their charm, warmth and lively conversation are well known. I have never met anyone so visually aware as Alberto. Added to this, his life-enhancing personality with its inner vibrancy and seeming youthfulness has made this an unforgettable project to work on.

CLARA YOUNG
Keeper of Art
City of Dundee District Council
May 1993

FOREWORD

If you come across one of Alberto Morrocco's paintings in a gallery or a private house, or if you are sitting in a meeting in a boardroom and you are lucky enough to have one of his portraits to share the tedium with you, there is never any mistake about who painted the picture. If this is so, it is not because his pictures are repetitive. Nor is it because of any quirk of style, or oddity of approach. It is because his painting is warm, generous and immediate and in the painting one recognises the man. That these pictures are also highly accomplished and in the best sense professional does not diminish their immediacy in the least, and this too reflects the man. His pictures have the poise that comes from well-founded confidence.

It was as a pupil of James Cowie and Robert Sivell in Aberdeen that the foundations of Alberto Morrocco's art were laid, and this places him in a very particular tradition of Scottish art. Appropriately for a Scots-Italian, too, it is one that is profoundly in sympathy with the older traditions of Italian art and he has maintained and developed the passion and professionalism that he learnt from his teachers in a way that has left its mark on art in Scotland. During the long period that he was Head of Painting at Duncan of Jordanstone College of Art, through his teaching and example, he has left generations of students in his debt.

For many of the rest of us, it is above all for his portraiture that we owe him gratitude. He has reinvigorated an art form, the professional portrait, that one would have been excused for thinking moribund, if not actually extinct. In the interview with Clara Young that makes up the main part of this book, he describes how he painted one of his finest portraits, that of Lord Cameron, in Raeburn's studio, and this seems entirely appropriate.

Nevertheless, as this retrospective will clearly show, it would seriously misrepresent Alberto Morrocco's achievement to praise him as a portrait painter alone. In the two texts which make up this book, Victoria Keller's outline of the development of the artist's painting and the fascinating conversation with Clara Young, it is always his dedication to the whole art of painting that shows through. It is this which is so fittingly celebrated in his retrospective exhibition and in this book.

DUNCAN MACMILLAN
April 1993

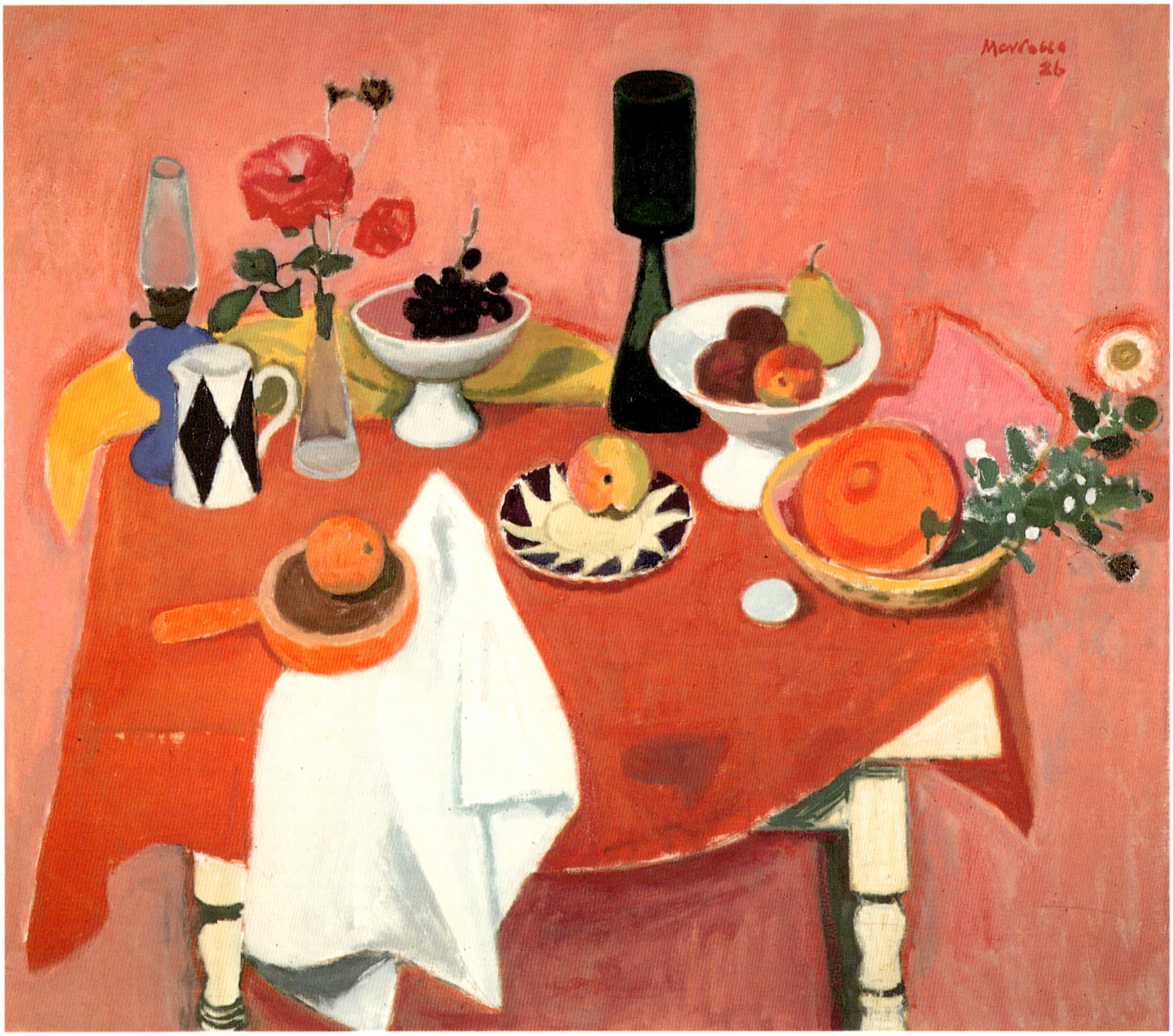

Plate 1 *Still-life on Red Cloth*, 1986 (Cat. 140)

A RETROSPECTIVE

When I began the research for Alberto Morrocco's first major career retrospective exhibition, I knew very little about the man or his life's work. Most of my everyday work had been, for a number of years, with young artists only a few years out of art college. Now I was being invited to look into the work of one of their teachers, someone who for over thirty years had been responsible for training young artists. It was fascinating to find that Alberto Morrocco was also, of course, taught and that he was influenced by his teachers. Like his own students, he had then to find his own way, to discover his own style through his own experience of life. This he did and is still doing. This essay is an attempt to give an overview of Alberto Morrocco's artistic progress from his time as a student to the present day, wherein we see an artist whose work is still developing and who is continuing to find fresh things to say about colour, shape and form, and love of life.

The exhibition and this book are an attempt, with the artist's collaboration, to convey the breadth of Alberto Morrocco's development as an artist over the past sixty years. This has taken him from the fastidious draughtsmanship of his college days to being called an inheritor of the Scottish Colourist tradition. The latter is true in as much as Morrocco's use of colour over the past twenty-five years has become more heated as well as abstracted from reality. He did not, however, pick up on this tradition in his early career. On the contrary, as we will see, he came to the use of hot, emotive colour over a very long period, which took him to some of the same sources as those of the Scottish Colourists. His conclusions, however, are not really the same, in spite of his use of strong colour – possibly because his beginnings in art were of a very different order.

To Alberto Morrocco the fine craft of picture-making has always been as important as the selection of his subject matter. His training was based upon an almost Italian Renaissance emphasis on the importance of preliminary drawing and the well-structured composition of a painting. This approach has been employed by the artist in a stylistic development stretching over sixty years, with subject matter ranging from domestic genre scenes to visions of Italian life, from still-life to commissioned portraiture. On occasion his stylistic approach has varied according to the needs, as he sees it, of differing subject matter. The ability to work in this way comes from Morrocco's art college training in Aberdeen in the 1930s. The desire to explore different approaches within contemporaneous material is a fundamental part of his belief in the 'renaissance man': that is to say, someone who is fluent in various means of expression.

Morrocco trained at Gray's School of Art in Aberdeen from 1932 until 1938, studying under James Cowie (1886-1956) and Robert Sivell (1888-1958), at the time when D. M. Sutherland (1883-1973) was the Principal of the school. Cowie and Sivell had both studied at Glasgow School of Art in the early years of the century, when Maurice Greiffenhagen was Master in Charge of the Life Department. The teachers at Glasgow, until well into the 1920s, tended to teach a hard-edged figurative style informed by the Pre-Raphaelitism of the nineteenth century and a deep love of the Italian Quattrocento. The attention to fine draughtsmanship that was so important to Cowie has stayed with Morrocco throughout his career. In *Still-life with Plaster*

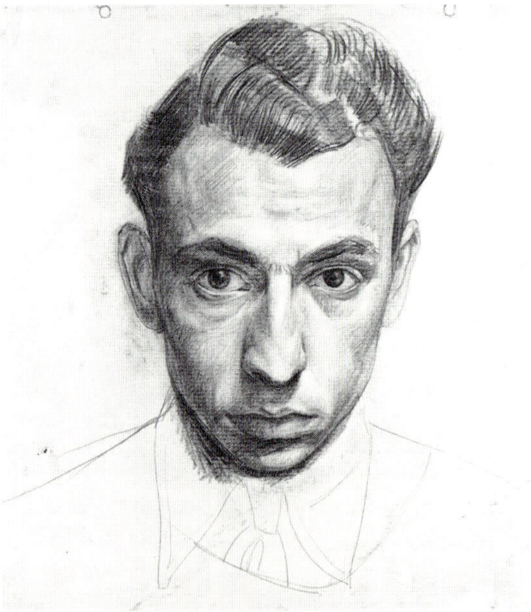

Plate 2 *Self-portrait*, *c*.1935 (Cat.2)

Cast and Measuring Tape (Pl.4), *c*.1935, which was painted under Cowie's direct tutelage, it is also possible to detect that cool, surreal quality that was the hallmark of so much of Cowie's work. Robert Sivell's overwhelming interest in Italian Renaissance art also made a lasting impression on Morrocco. Sivell's distaste for contemporary art was well known and he vigorously taught in the time-honoured tradition of encouraging his students to paint in the styles of the old masters in order to learn their craft. Sivell's own stylistic approach had its influence on Morrocco for some time as well, with his insistence on a very limited palette and his resistance to the modern art of the time. Its final appearance can be seen most strongly in some of Morrocco's commissioned portraits of the mid-1950s, with their silvery tones, and in the monochromatic nature of much of his work until the 1960s.

The Second World War began just as Morrocco was finishing his student travels on the continent. He began exhibiting regularly at the Royal Scottish Academy from 1939 onwards and the works painted during the war years are of subjects harking back to his pre-war travels in France (he has always been a prodigious sketcher and has developed subjects in his paintings from drawings made many years previously), as well as occasional self-portraits, portraits of his wife Vera and his children, Aberdeen street scenes and portraits of soldiers and, by 1946, military hospital scenes. *Holland Place, Sunday Evening (Pl.10)*, from *c*.1949-50, is a typical broadly painted work, rich in ochres. Holland Place was where the Morrocco family lived in Aberdeen and the artist produced a number of low-keyed sketches at the time.

Morrocco's work of the 1940s stays close stylistically to his art college roots – an avoidance of the international avant-garde art of his time such as the Ecole de Paris and American abstract expressionism. Though his sketches were broadly painted, his more finished works employed a flatter handling, and the work of the late 1940s employs a kind of realism in sympathy with the social realism of a certain strand of British art of the time. A work from 1950-51 in Aberdeen Art Gallery, *A Winter Morning (Pl.13)*, exemplifies this period and could be compared to the work of his older contemporary, McIntosh Patrick. It is panoramic in its intentions, and is highly detailed with a very crisply handled paint surface. Also at this time, along with colleagues from Gray's where he was teaching part-time, he collaborated on the 950 illustrations for the book, *Anatomy of the Human Body*, written by Professor Lockhart and colleagues from Aberdeen University. Page upon page of highly detailed pictures of muscles and bones, it is a monument to the style of training these artists underwent in their day and was intended for use by artists, medical students and laymen alike.

While a picture resulting from Morrocco's first trip to Spain in the early 1950s, *Sun Worshippers (Pl.20)*, is the first in a very long line of beach scenes, it gives little indication of the effect the light and colour of Spain and Italy would have upon his art in the mid-1950s. By the time this picture was painted in 1954, its meticulous

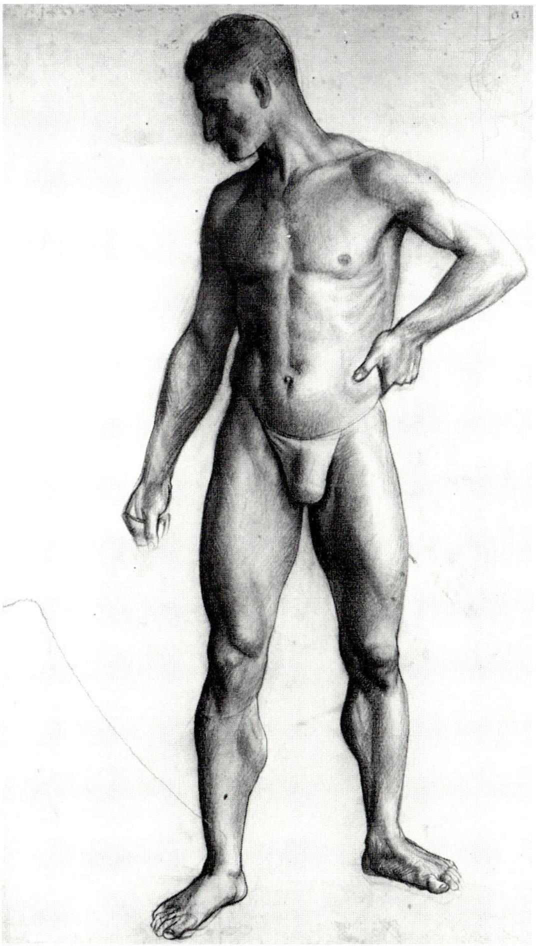

Plate 3 *Male Model – Study*, c.1935 (Cat.3)

approach using classical modelling and subdued tones, was giving way to an avid exploration of colour. Whether this change was related to his discovery of the warmth of the colours of Italy and Spain, to his new job as Head of Drawing and Painting at Dundee's Duncan of Jordanstone College of Art that he had taken up in 1950 and which brought him into contact with new colleagues and new ideas, or even possibly to the after-effects of the 1948 Vuillard and Bonnard exhibition at the Edinburgh International Festival, it is hard to say. Whatever the case, in the 1950s, Morrocco produced a series of paintings of domestic scenes as well as landscapes that owe a great deal to a study of Vuillard. The flat handling has become broken into neo-impressionist dabs of colour that cover the entire picture surface. For example, as in *The Mantelpiece (Vera) (Pl.17)* of 1953, the subjects of these pictures reflect a pleasure in family life and a discovery of landscape that must have demanded of the artist a new mood in his art. With this stylistic change the artist begins to introduce a new, more buoyant attitude to colour in his work. He moved away from the restricted palette he had imposed upon himself as a result of his training. There is no doubt, though, that these pictures were prepared for as carefully as those that preceded them

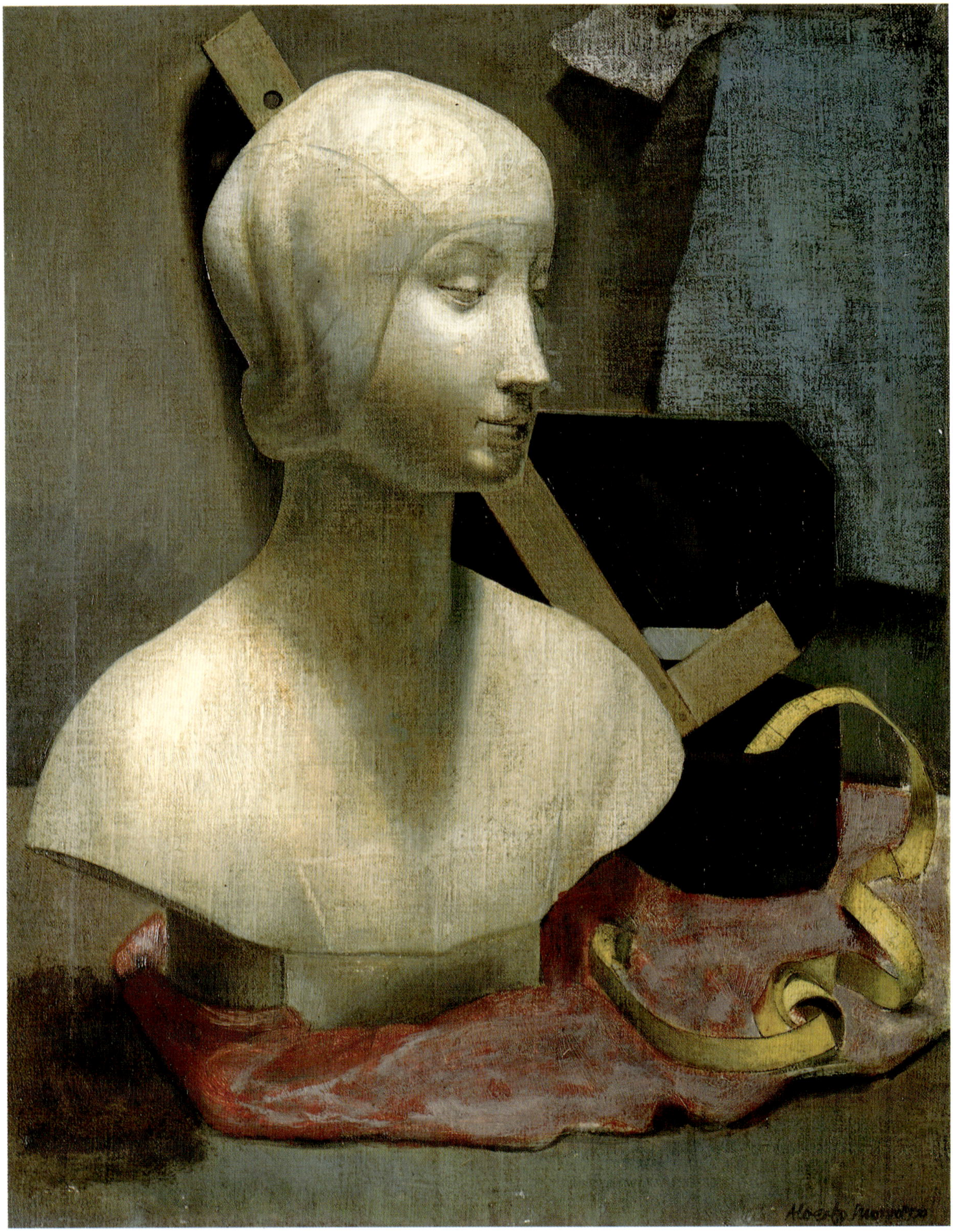

Plate 4 *Still-life with Plaster Cast and Measuring Tape*, c.1935 (Cat.5)

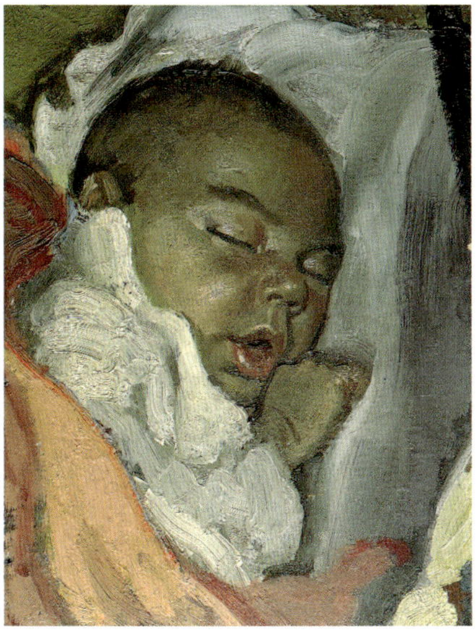

Plate 5 *Brown Baby Laurie*, 1947 (Cat.10)

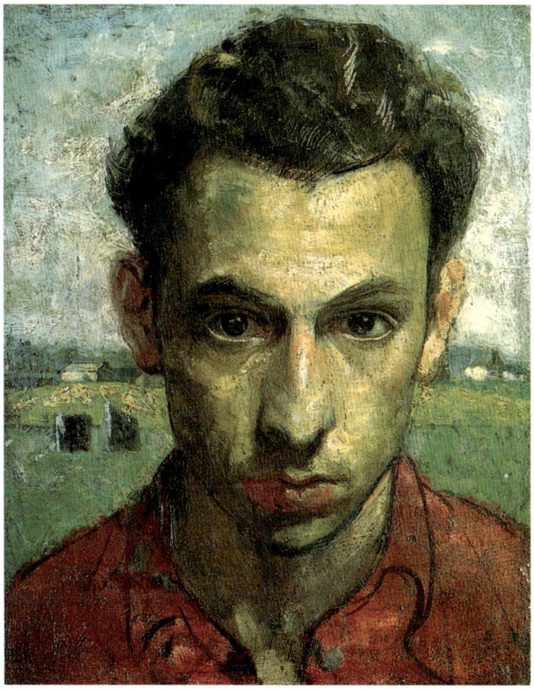

Plate 6 *Self-portrait at 17 Years*, c.1935 (Cat.1)

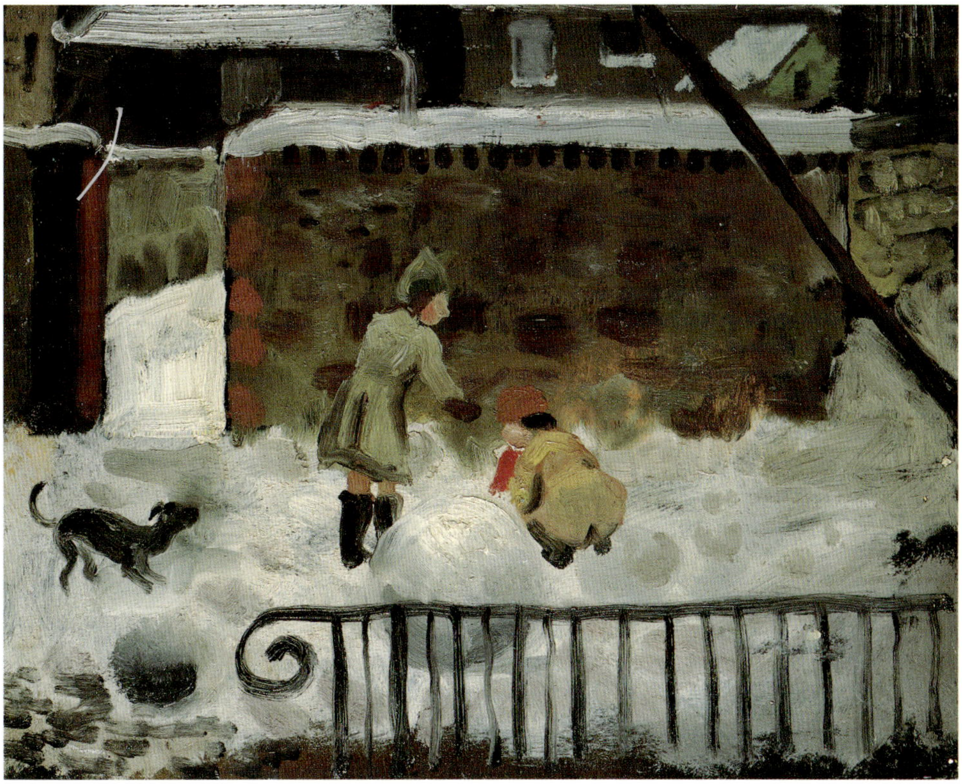

Plate 7 *Winter in Holland Place*, 1949 (Cat.13)

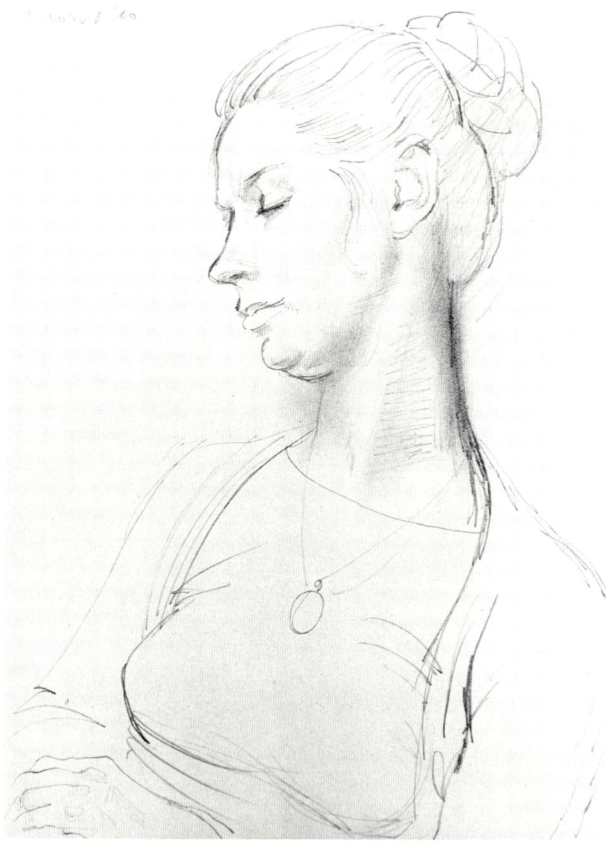

Plate 8 *Vera*, c.1947 (Cat.11)

and those that followed, but the response to new stimuli required a handling that called upon a seemingly more spontaneous, joyous, and certainly more sensuous approach.

It is during the 1950s that Morrocco's work begins to show the diversity of approach for which he has sometimes been criticised. His commissioned portraits begin to diverge stylistically from the rest of his art at this time. Throughout the 1950s and early 1960s, they hark back to Robert Sivell's influence, with their silvery tones and rather flat handling of paint. The portrait styles continued not to relate to his contemporaneous handling of other subject matter until well into the 1970s, when one style began more consistently to inform all the areas of his production.

By the late 1950s and early 1960s, Morrocco had developed all the thematic subject matter that has become associated with his work. Most of the important themes relate to his experiences of Italy and Spain: glimpses through mysterious half-open doors which might be either house entrances or confessionals in shadowy churches; women leaning out of upper windows for a gossip; women doing chores; families and horseback riders on the beach; wistful clowns and moody-looking fortune-tellers and the ever present landscape of Italy and its streets and buildings, shores and mountains.

Morrocco's style of the late 1950s began to show a greater simplification in depicting the human form. The broken neo-impressionist handling gave way to strongly contoured chunky figures of Sicilian women going about their daily routine. Sometimes these powerful figures are highlighted using outlines, sometimes

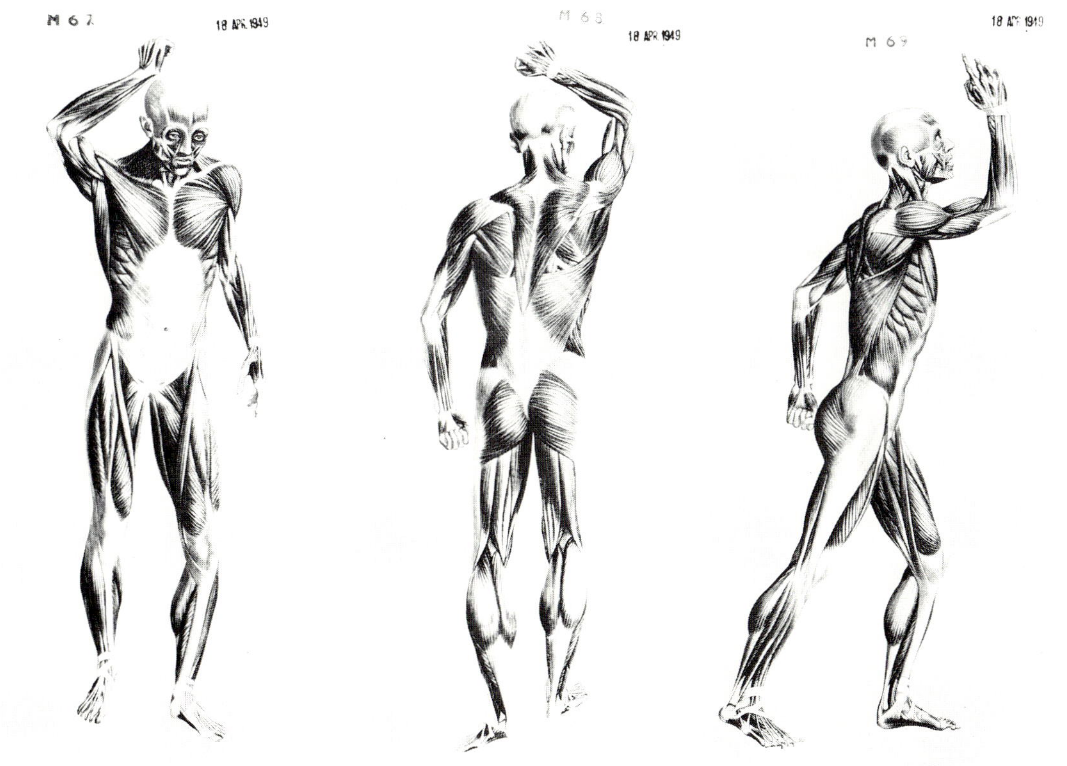

Plate 9 *Three Vesalius Figures for* Anatomy of the Human Body, c.1948 (Cat.12)

not. *I Poveri* (*c*.1957) was used as a study for the much larger *I Poveri (Pl.27)* of 1959. The former is a very dark, tightly worked little picture which the artist allowed to grow into a grander scale, more schematically painted. The colour key remains somewhat muted, but he had begun the grand simplification of the objects of his study, which he carried on throughout the next three decades. This deliberate inclination towards archaic shapes owes something to the artist's admiration of Picasso, but also, perhaps, to Italian artists such as Marino Marini. The latter's paintings and sculptures of clowns, horseback riders and statuesque women were well known in Italy and abroad certainly throughout the 1950s and 1960s. However, the sympathetic direction of Morrocco's paintings of poor people in Sicily in the late 1950s are in step with Renato Guttuso's Italian brand of social realism which was known in Britain from the early 1950s.

The following decade was a time of major experimentation for Morrocco. This is all the more remarkable when one remembers that he was teaching full-time, heading a department, and was already at an age when many less adventurous artists would have comfortably settled into a life-long style. This was an incredibly fertile time for the arts. Abstract expressionism had been a powerful force in the 1950s and was still going strong in the early 1960s. Pop art had fully arrived on the scene and new ideas in art and music were coming thick and fast, especially within the context of Britain's art schools. Morrocco's landscapes of the early 1960s reflect the ferment of the times and are probably as close as the artist will ever get to abstract expressionism. *Setting Sun II (Pl.39)*, of *c*.1962, and *Hill Village and Monastery* (*c*.1963), (*Pl.42*), belong to a series of paintings of quarries or hills topped with villages or monasteries in which the artist

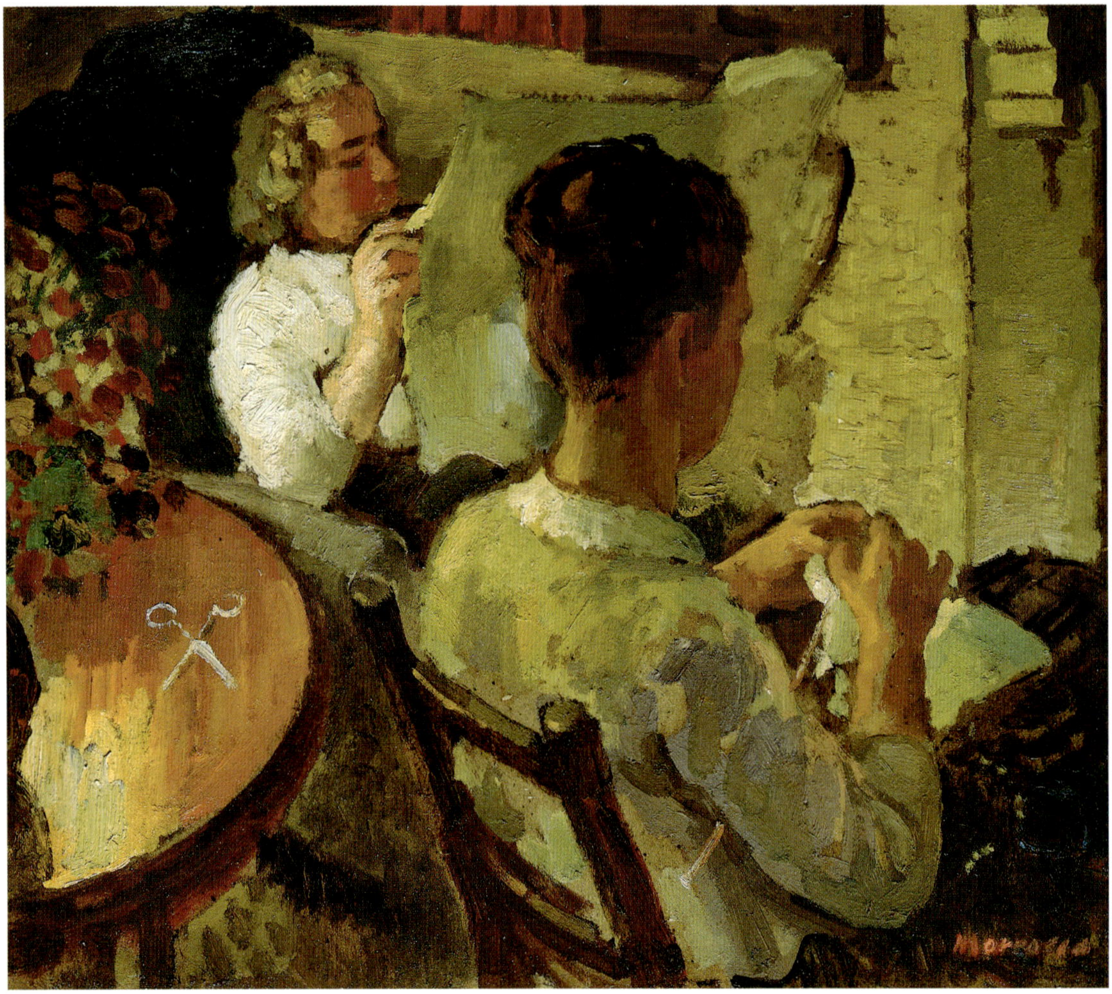

Plate 10 *Holland Place, Sunday Evening (Vera and Celesta)*, c.1949/50 (Cat.15)

has employed an excited brushwork, laying the paint on heavily and frequently allowing it to drip down the surface of the canvas. Though this phase was not of long duration, it does show that Morrocco was open to new ideas, and willing to try them out in his own work with some success.

Morrocco also produced a large number of three-dimensional works in the 1960s. There is a series of built-up pictures, almost like collages – large, heavy works, several of doorways – that bring the subject right into the viewer's space. There is an even larger number of sculptures. Exhibited at Glasgow's Compass Gallery in 1969, these were frequently asssembled out of found objects, often from beaches in Italy. The works are quirky and humorous, reminiscent of the amusing, sometimes slightly threatening found-object sculptures that Picasso and Miró produced of surreal people and animals.

Another area of new work was the production of large-scale murals. While still a student, Morrocco had assisted Robert Sivell on a large mural which is still to be found in the Students' Union in Aberdeen. During the early to mid-1960s, Morrocco worked on an immense mural of Christ carrying the Cross for St Columba's Church in Glenrothes, and he painted two large murals for Liff Hospital in Dundee. These

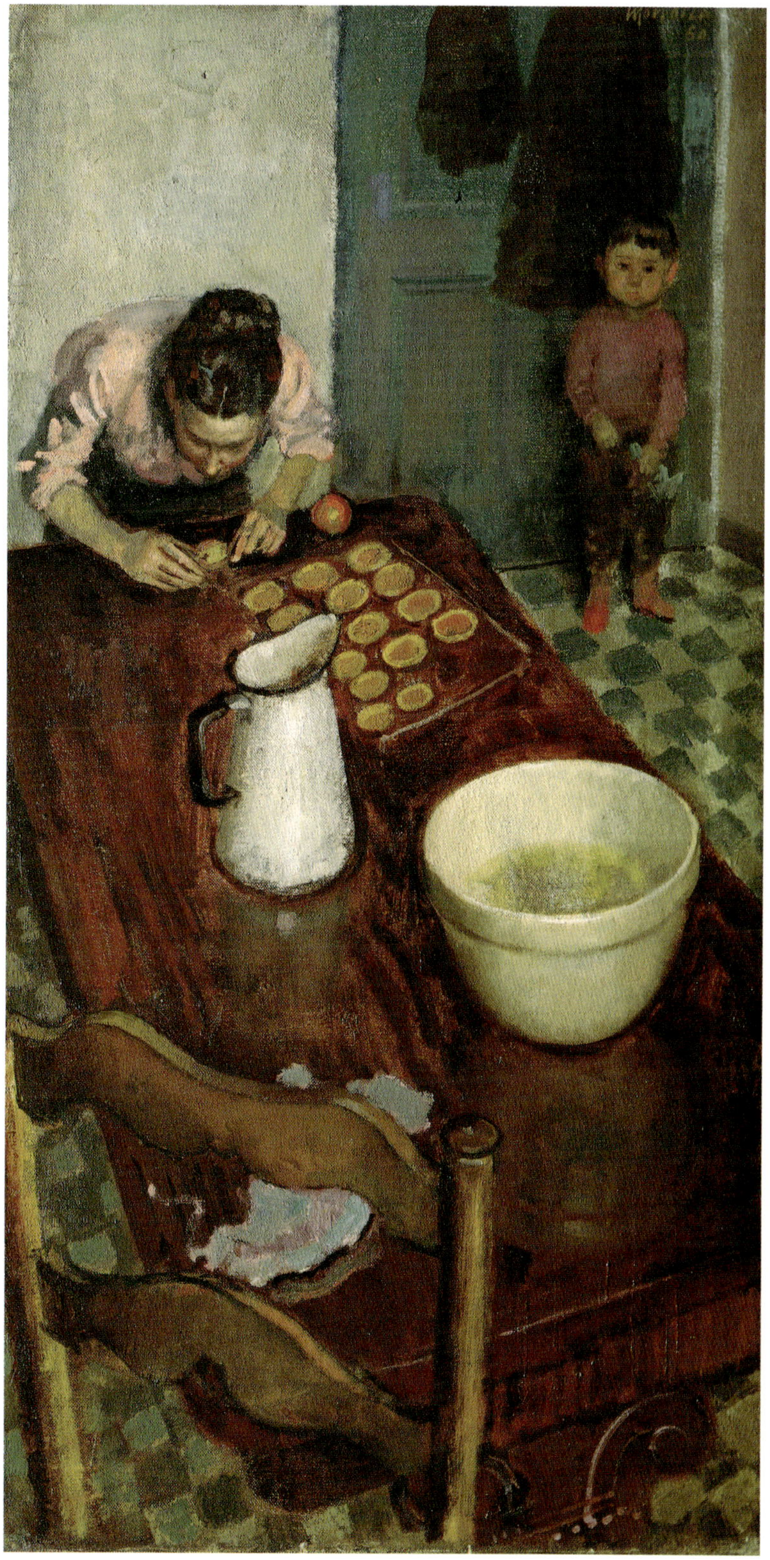

Plate 11 *Baking Cakes*, 1947-50 (Cat.17)

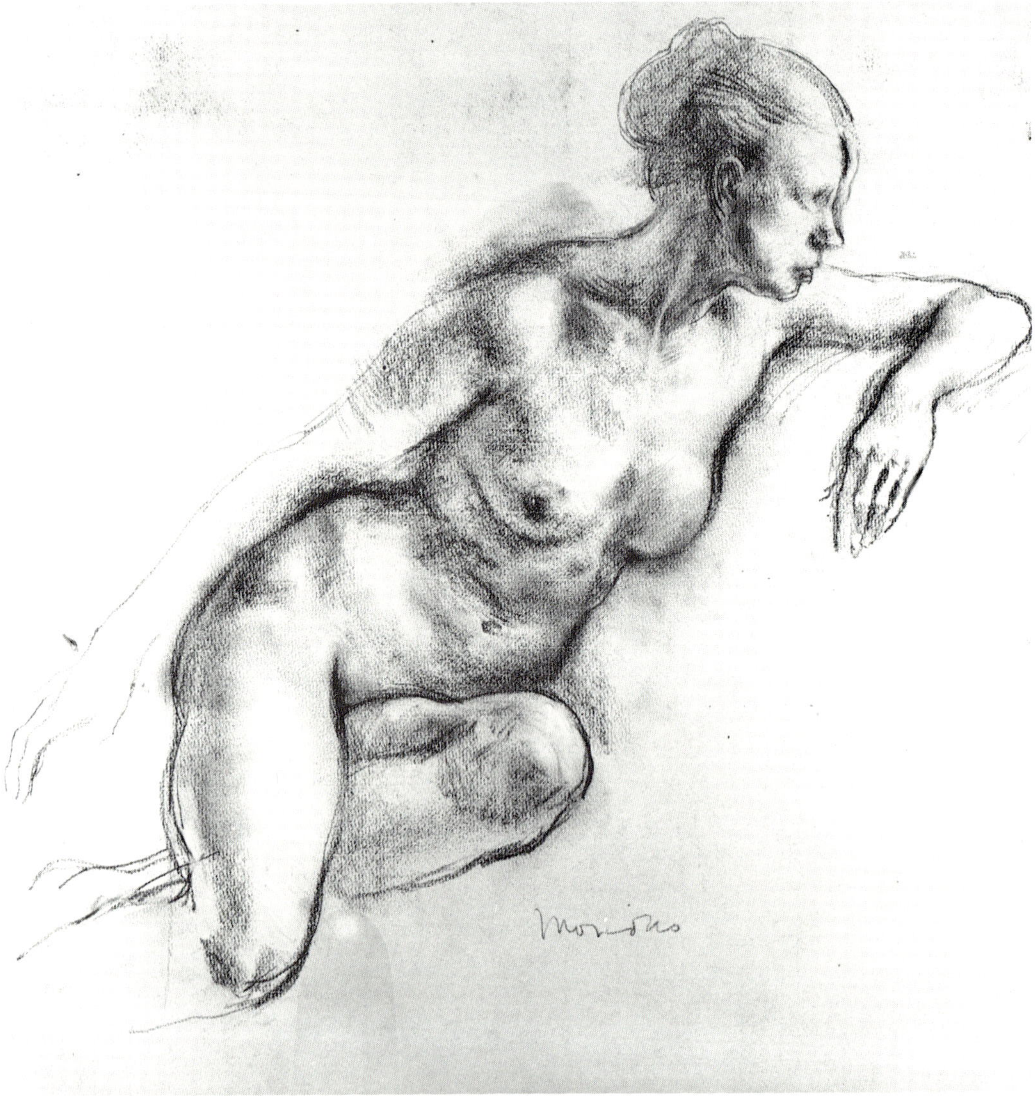

Plate 12 *Nude Study – Vera,* 1949 (Cat.14)

enabled him to consolidate his earlier experiences at Aberdeen while being in control stylistically of a medium he was fascinated by through its links to Italian Renaissance art.

By the late 1960s and early 1970s, Morrocco's stylistic approach to still-life and Italian thematic subject matter had begun to crystallise into the recognisable Morrocco style of today. For example, *The Beach at Stromboli (Pl.53)*, c.1970, was followed by *Fine Day at the Lido (Pl.50)* and *Dull Day at the Lido (Pl.49)*, both from 1972. The former, while full of light, is still cautious in its use of colour. The latter two are explosive in contrast. While often basing his work then, as now, on sketches made years before, memory and mood began to play a greater part in his handling of colour. Powerful and warm colours, dictated by mood and memory rather than nature, started to dominate all his work, allied with the powerful contours which had displaced straight classical forms in the late 1950s. While the impasto never returned to the richness of the early 1960s, it is finely modelled and never really flat. From the early 1960s onwards, Morrocco's Scottish subject matter lost ground in comparison to his subjects based on his experiences of southern climates. Scottish landscapes such as 1977's *Tay Bridge, Winter* are primarily winter scenes with snow, where the northern coldness of light works well and the pictures are nearly monochrome, while the brightly heated colours are reserved for the subject matter of southern climates. The pictures become increasingly decorative with time, in that the pleasure is as much derived from the balance and quality of the colour as from the subject matter. This is a kind of hedonism, a love of rich patterning and a sensuous delight in colour which came to many artists such as Matisse and Paul Klee amongst others, as well as – farther back – Delacroix and all those more or less northern artists who made the discovery of extremely hot climates, Mediterranean light and their effect upon colour.

A good example of how the artist has developed his themes can be seen specifically in his pictures of Venice. In 1973 Morrocco took a sabbatical trip to Venice in order to paint a 'portrait of the city'. Out of this trip came a multitude of drawings, watercolours and oil paintings of churches and piazzas and buildings along the canals, mostly without figures. Since much of his time on that trip was spent during the winter, the colour of the immediate paintings from that trip is subdued, while being very much in the style of the time – worked in patchwork blocks of colour, structured within powerful contours. The drawings from that trip have, however, provided the artist with picture material ever since then and the colours of paintings made ten years later have become stronger and more vibrant – a matter of personal choice according to mood.

From the mid-1970s onwards, an aspect of Morrocco's work that has gained strength continuously is the still-life. Part of his art college training would have been in making pictures of still-lifes, and he has painted them since the 1930s. Those of the 1950s were part of his intimate Vuillard-like interiors. Until Morrocco acknowledged the necessity to himself of the use of sensuous Mediterranean colour in his still-lifes, his work in this area in the 1960s was overshadowed by his experience of abstract expressionism – heavily painted, often overpainted and usually sombrely coloured. By the 1970s, he had developed a solid, more sculptural and archaic modelling that had influenced his figurative subjects for some time. By the middle of the decade his use of colour was definitely heating up, with a nod particularly in the direction of Matisse's interiors and odalisques. The *Grande Natura Morta Napolitana (Pl.66)* of 1975, with its overtones of seventeenth-century still-life painting and extremely restrained, highly elegant handling, rushes headlong into *Turcomania (Pl.70)* of 1976, as if he intended to get stuck in with a vengeance to the heated colours of the next seventeen years. When that happened his still-lifes began to achieve an assurance they had sometimes lacked until then. But people matter to Morrocco's art and even in his still-lifes, figures creep in, or their actions are left behind, such as a knife left quivering in the top of a table or sticking into a water-melon. The paintings of the 1980s and 1990s show the increasing importance of the still-life as something of an excuse for an almost abstract balancing act for the multiple use of strong colours, which clash cheerfully with each other at every opportunity.

By the 1960s, during the stylistic upheavals in his other areas of work, Morrocco was searching for a new style in his commissioned portrait work. He was much in demand for his work in this area throughout the 1960s, 1970s and 1980s. His pictures of the early 1960s show less illusionistic modelling than those of the previous decade, which were still painted under Robert Sivell's influence. In drawing away from Sivell, he began to simplify his paintwork, while still keeping everything tied together with a linear

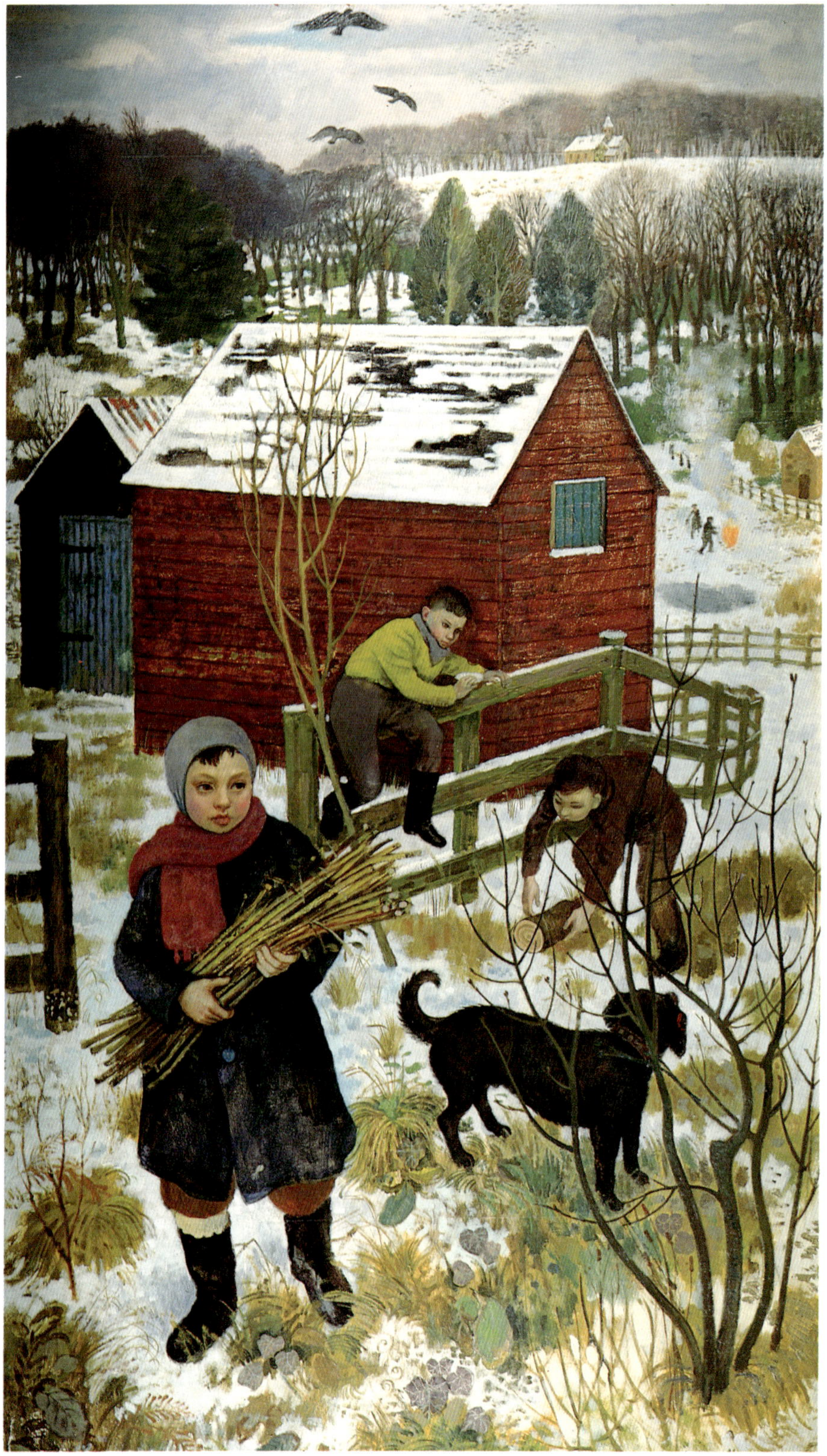

Plate 13 *A Winter Morning*, 1951 (Cat.23)

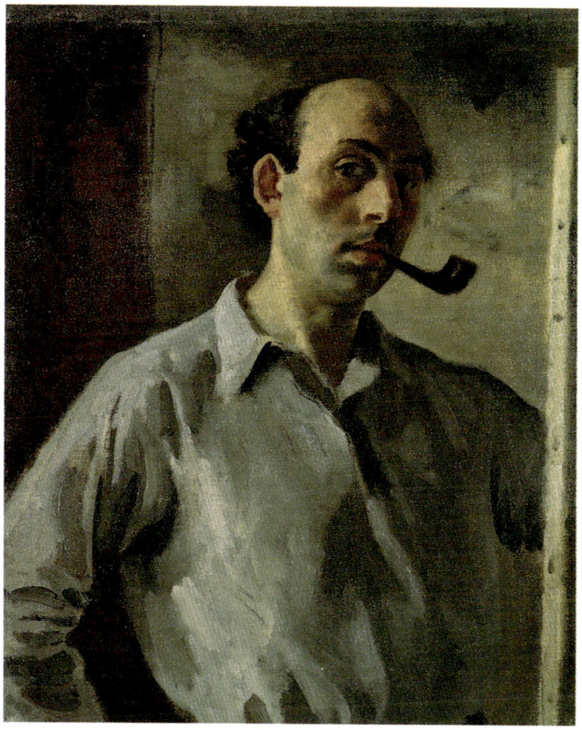

Plate 14 *Self-portrait, c.*1952 (Cat.24)

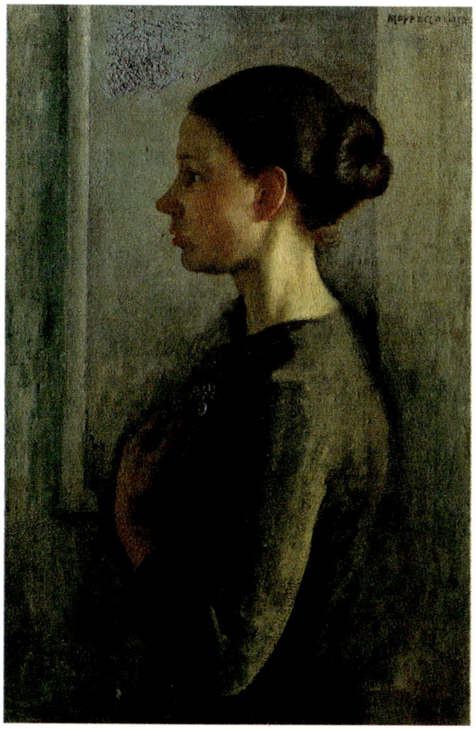

Plate 15 *Profile in Grey (Vera)*, 1952 (Cat.26)

structure. In leaving behind some of the concessions to naturalism of the 1950s, he began to look towards a rather more schematic rendering while still doing his best to give a likeness in a sympathetic context. By the early 1970s he was searching for inspiration as far back in Scottish portraiture history as Raeburn when he painted *The Hon Lord Cameron (Pl.65)* for the University of Edinburgh in Raeburn's own studio in Edinburgh (1974). In 1992 Morrocco painted a portrait of *Sir Anthony Wheeler (Pl.88)*, which had been commissioned by the Royal Scottish Academy. This picture is clearly part of Morrocco's work of the 1990s. It is painted within the parameters of a Morrocco still-life in which a person actually takes pride of place. It is less schematic, certainly, than those still-lifes, but that is the artist's concession to commissioned recognisability. The handling is the same though the colour is not keyed as high as his current work. This is because the picture is from life, painted inside the RSA building under artificial light. The artist has kept himself in check due to circumstance; the result is friendly but elegant, somewhere in between a portrait such as *Lord Cameron* and a picture of a family member.

From the 1970s to the 1990s Morrocco has consolidated his work stylistically. He has travelled a great deal and this has led to a greater variety of subject matter and, if that were possible, to a greater explosion of colour. The handling of the paint has stayed somewhat flat though well modelled, the contours remain clear and confident, occasionally outlined to make them more powerful – all part of the process begun in the late 1950s. He has very occasionally reverted stylistically to earlier approaches, and when this does occur, it is usually in the context of remembering a past time in terms of the style of that time.

While Alberto Morrocco is firmly a part of the Scottish tradition in art, he does not belong to that part known to many as the Edinburgh 'painterly' school of largely French-inspired attitudes to painting, where some might place him due to his love of colour. He actually belongs to that strongly graphic tradition in painting which Cowie and Sivell took to Aberdeen from the Glasgow School of Art of the early twentieth century. Morrocco took this tradition with him to Duncan of Jordanstone College of Art in Dundee where he was Head of Drawing and Painting for over thirty years. Undoubtedly he influenced the selection of teaching staff in that time and this has given Duncan of Jordanstone's students a reputation for a strongly graphic strength underlying their art which has impressed observers of contemporary Scottish art for quite some time.

To that graphic strength gained in his own art school days Morrocco has brought a delight in the southern light and brilliant colour of his Italian ancestry. Through many years of experimentation and development he has forged his own art of mood and sensation that, on the one hand, reflects a solidity of approach in the construction of his art and, on the other hand, an exuberance and joyfulness in the warm colours of his creation.

VICTORIA KELLER
March 1993

ALBERTO MORROCCO IN CONVERSATION

The text which follows is from two conversations between Clara Young and Alberto Morrocco which were recorded at his home in Dundee. The first, a wide-ranging and informal interview, took place on 4 March 1993; the second, which was much more structured with questions on specific paintings and Alberto's views on art, was held on 24 March 1993, and begins on page 50.

BACKGROUND

CLARA: *Let's just start with this question. How do you feel about this retrospective exhibition that we are organising for you?*

ALBERTO: I find it a traumatic experience to be absolutely honest, because it's like baring your soul for public examination and, going back as far as this is going – I don't know how to describe it really – I find it a bit awful actually. I remember talking to Keith Vaughan some years ago. He told me that after he'd had his retrospective in the Whitechapel Gallery, he couldn't paint for two years afterwards. The fact that he saw his whole life – his whole career – placed out before him on the walls . . . he hadn't realised the kind of development he'd made and how things had been changing. That upset him and I can understand now why.

Last night you opened the exhibition of the Scottish Colourists at Stirling University. You have been described as the 'last Scottish Colourist'.

Have I?

Or in a Scottish Colourist tradition. What do you say to that?

Well, I don't think that is altogether true. Somebody once said that to me before. You see, I said in my little speech last night that I admired the Scottish Colourists for their interesting work but that I admired more the *source* of their inspiration, which was Manet, Monet, Matisse – not Picasso so much, although I admire Picasso – but that group of French painters around the turn of the century. I've never actually felt that I was directly influenced by any of the Colourists, Peploe or Cadell or any of them. But I could admit to being influenced by Matisse, of course, and by Picasso.

We will go back and talk a bit about the family. You are often described as an Italo-Scot. Do you feel Scottish or Italian?

You're asking some difficult questions. I feel Italian to be perfectly honest but I cannot claim to be a true Italian in the sense of being an Italian who was born and brought up in Italy and who speaks the language fluently, because it is a native language. I am not that kind of an Italian; you see, it's a hybrid I am really, which is an odd kind of thing. But I did have an Italian upbringing, albeit in Aberdeen. My whole background was related to being thought of as an Italian and that carries on being so. In all honesty I cannot think of myself as a true Scot either, you see, because I have no Scottish blood to begin with and I have often different emotional reactions to a given situation. I used to feel it quite strongly occasionally in the art college [Duncan of Jordanstone] with teaching mainly Scottish students. Often I came to a point in discussion in which I saw the difference in opinion was something to do with a kind of racial background difference. It's a curious mixture – I am not a real Italian and certainly not a Scot.

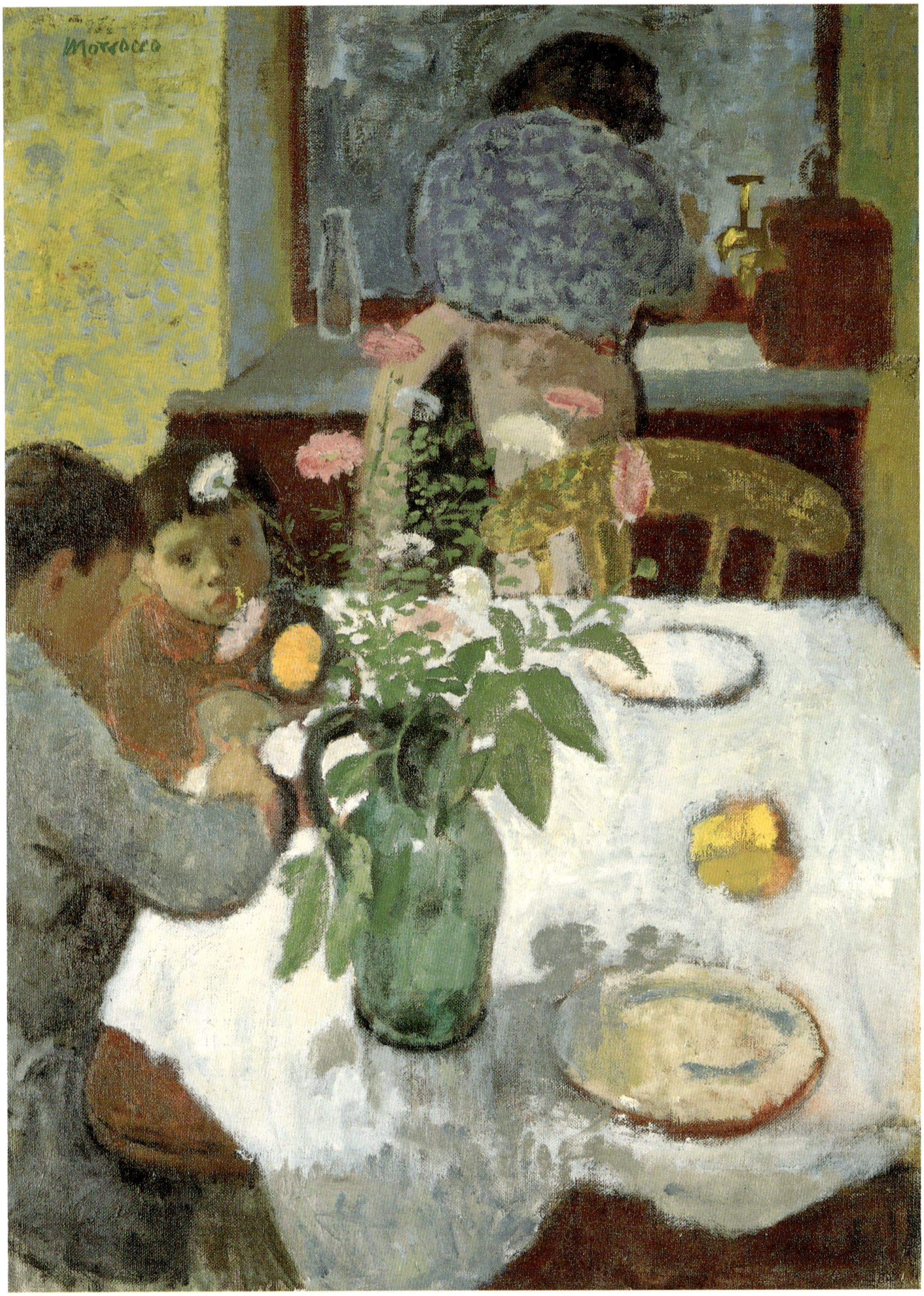

Plate 16 *The Boys in the Kitchen*, c.1952 (Cat.25)

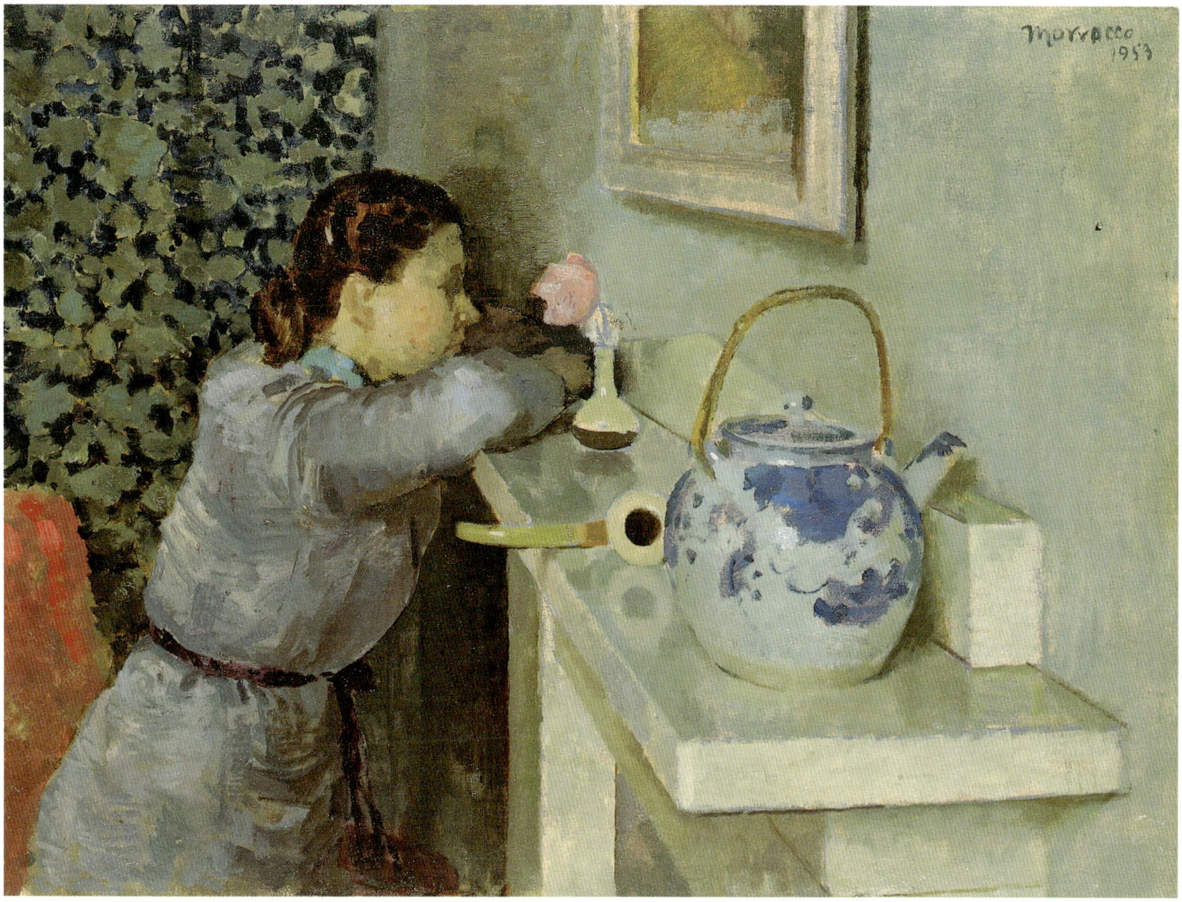

Plate 17 *The Mantelpiece (Vera)*, 1953 (Cat.27)

That's fascinating – the racial or national background. Can you pinpoint the different characteristics?

Well, can you actually establish a national characteristic? I suppose the Italian thing is more emotional – I suppose that's fairly true. It is also maybe slightly more superficial, as I have to admit. There is a certain superficiality in Italian cultural life. The Scottish character is maybe stronger and less imaginative – less given to flights of fancy, if you like to call it that – although these generalisations are perhaps too simplistic. But the national characteristics are certainly different. Although my parents . . . my father came to Aberdeen and fitted in very well. He was a Southern Italian. He wasn't the kind of ebullient Roman waiter type Italian who's full of the *joie de vivre* and so forth. He was rather a serious man, my father, but *simpatico*. He actually fitted in very well to the Scottish environment.

Your parents were both born in Italy. Could you tell me a bit about their background and how they came to Scotland?

My mother, Celesta Crolla, was brought to Scotland with her family, a big family from Southern Italy from a little village called Fontetuno which is right up near the top of a mountain. They came in three stages. She came in, I think, the second wave – she was only three years old. Now, that's

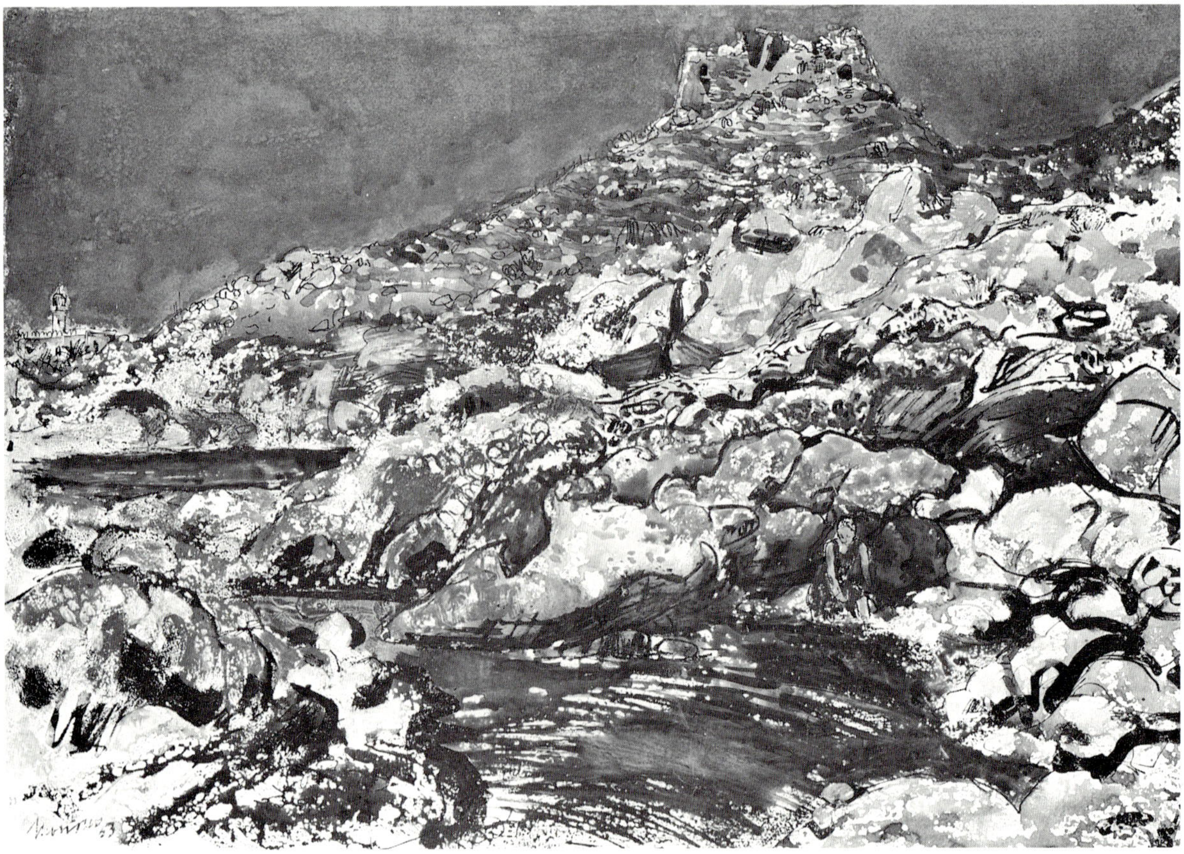

Plate 18 *Castle at Rosas*, 1953 (Cat.28)

significant because she had all her education in Scotland, in Aberdeen. She spoke Scots. She also spoke dialect Italian but didn't like speaking it. I seldom heard her. She never spoke it to my father. He spoke broken English, of course, because he was twenty-one when he settled down here. So he was a typical immigrant, much more than my mother was. He came from a very, very poor family from the region of Casino, the town of Casino. It was another big family: he had two brothers and three or four sisters. He came because of poverty – that's the reason. The same with mother's family. It was a way of making a new life for themselves, you see.

Your father came with his parents then?

No, no, no. He had an older brother who'd gone before him to Aberdeen – that is how he landed up in Aberdeen, round about 1912 or something like that. So, I was brought up and so was my brother in this curious situation which is not typical of first-generation Italian families in this country, of being spoken to in Scots. My mother was the main influence because my father had a shop – a café – we lived above it. He worked a very, very long day – got up at six in the morning, came up to bed about twelve at night each day – an incredible pattern of existence he had. As a result, we only saw him at meal-times and so forth, he was always busy – so my mother was the one, you see, who was the biggest influence on both of us. Scottish was spoken the whole time. As a result of that neither of us speak Italian, which is not typical. All the families of my generation that we knew in Aberdeen, all the families spoke dialect Italian – as well as Scots of course. So that's a new rule, you see. I've tried over the years to learn Italian – on two or three occasions I have taken it up and then let it drop because painting is a terribly hard taskmaster . . . so I have a smattering only.

What was your father like? Your brother Val told me he was the local strongman.

That's true, he was – again this is typical of the Italians of that period – he was kind of macho. He was a small man, powerfully built because he had worked all his life on a smallholding – he was a shepherd really when he was a boy. He was very muscular and he used to do this arm wrestling thing in the shop at night. It's all gone now, the old café thing – it was sort of a local Italian social centre as well as an ice-cream shop or coffee shop or whatever – and after the doors were closed at night, maybe about 10.30 or so, the locals who were friendly with him used to stay on. First they would play the guitar and the mandolin, sing songs – mainly this happened at weekends and I was present at lots of these gatherings when I got a bit older – and then they would start arm-wrestling and feats of strength. My father's speciality was lifting a table. He had powerful jaws, very powerful masseter muscles and absolutely fantastic teeth – totally untouched by any dentist ever – and he used to clamp his teeth to the end of a table. It was a long table – people used to sit at it eating ice-cream or taking coffee – and he put his hands behind his back and lifted the whole table until the other end touched the ceiling. It was incredible, there's no question about it – and he was only about five feet five inches. He had worked hard all his life and he had kept himself fit. Unfortunately he died young – he was only forty-six when he died. That was in 1936 I think or 1937 – I can't remember now.

Anything more about your family life?

We ate Italian-style because my father did a lot of cooking – he was a good cook.

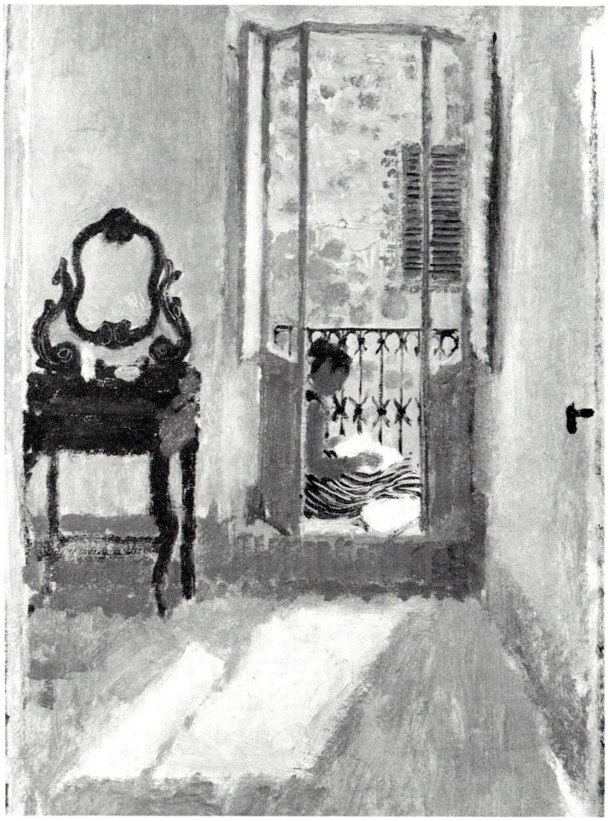

Plate 19 *The Blue Bedroom*, 1954 (Cat.38)

Did he make the ice-cream?

He made the ice-cream, of course – yes, he did everything in the shop down below but my mother wasn't a particularly dedicated cook herself. She was good with the frying pan but she wasn't keen on making sauces and all that kind of thing, so my father every so often used to do a bit of cooking himself – mainly during the winter when the season was quiet. He made spaghetti and so on – beef olives Italian-style – it was Italian-style food that we had at Christmas and those kind of periods. We had lots of visitors, Italian visitors – local ones. There was a typical kind of grapevine in Aberdeen of Italians who used to visit each other all the time – a constant stream of people of roughly my father's own generation coming round and chatting

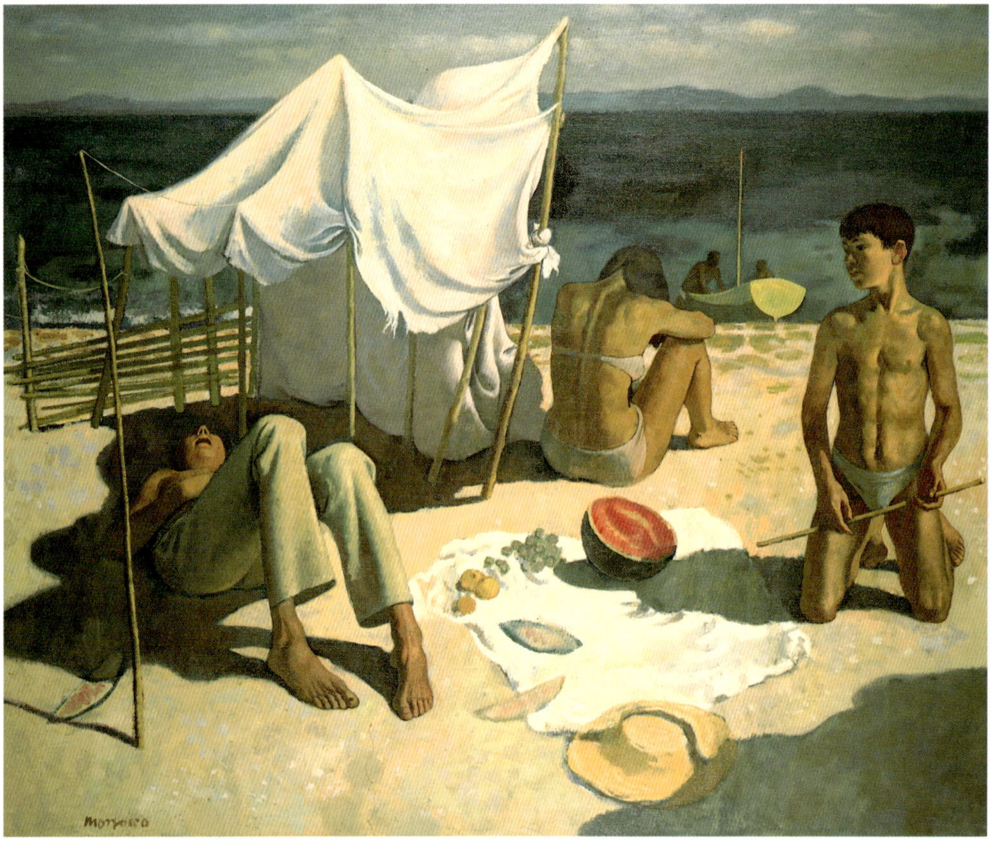

Plate 20 *Sun Worshippers*, 1954 (Cat.34)

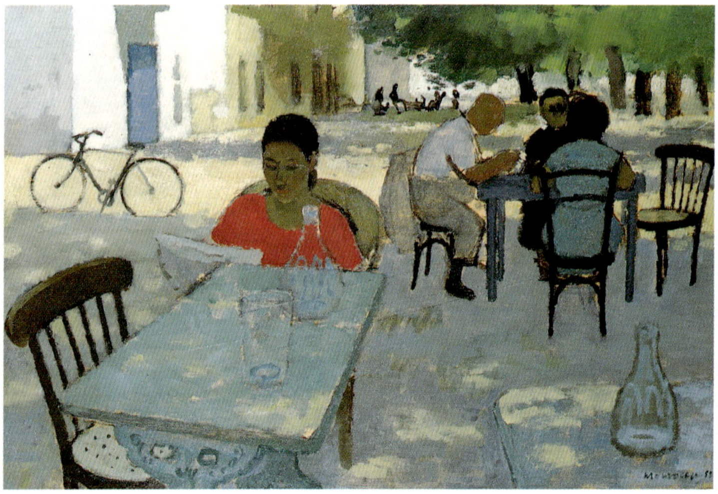

Plate 21 *Hotel Marina, Rosas*, 1953 (Cat.30)

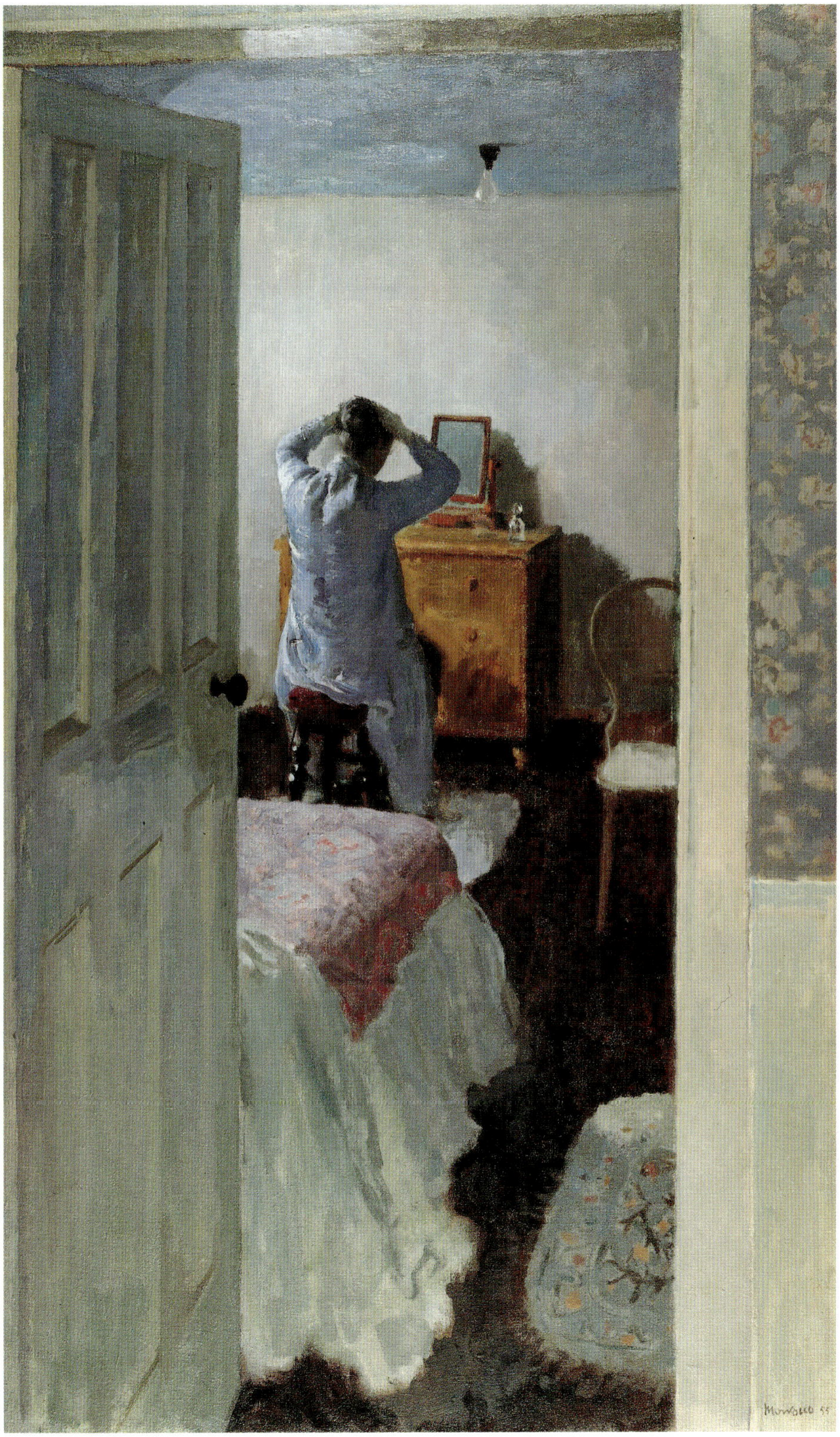

Plate 22 *The Attic Bedroom*, 1955 (Cat.40)

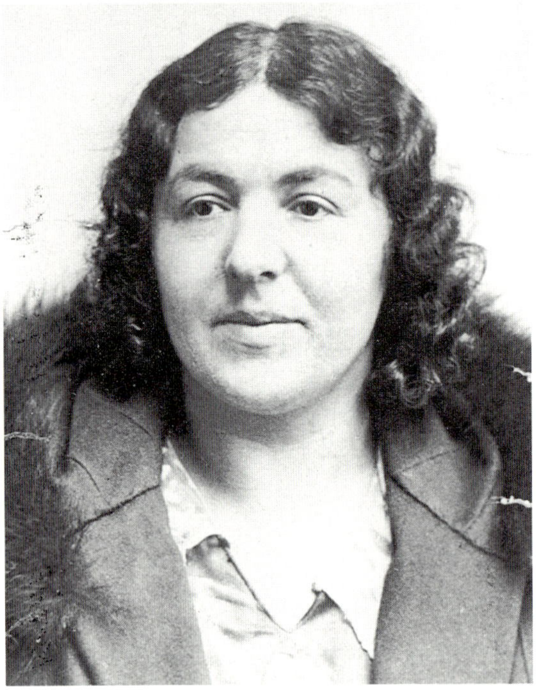

Plate 23 *Celesta Marrocco, the artist's mother*

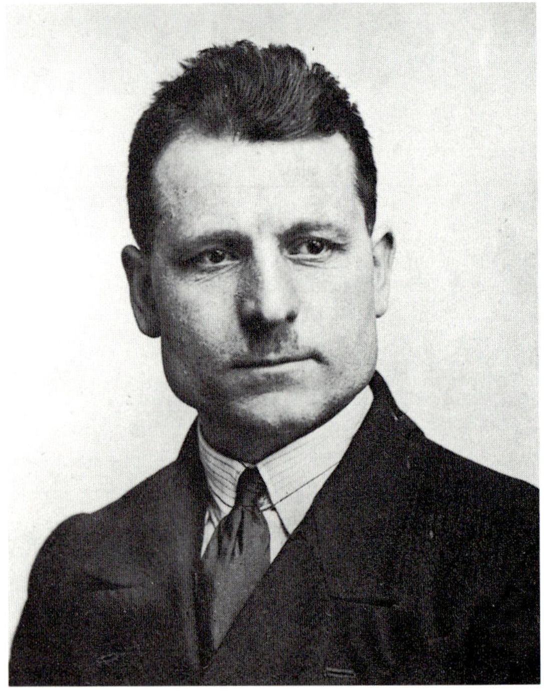

Plate 24 *Domenicantonio Marrocco, the artist's father*

about business and about family matters and about friends they'd seen and whether they had been to Italy, and what they had seen when they went back – this went on the whole time.

Things like Christmas were big occasions with Italians, I remember these very well and going to Midnight Mass – although neither of us was ever brought up with any religious persuasion, though we were nominally Catholics. My father had strong objections to the Catholic Church – it is quite typical in Italy to this day with the male of the species, a lot of them are not at all interested in the church. It's women who are actually the people you see in churches in Italy. Anyway, he never went or he stopped going. My mother occasionally went but she eventually stopped as well. I can remember when I was very young being taken but after that I stopped too and so we – my brother and I – had no religious upbringing of any kind. So I have still to this day, you see, no affiliation to any church – nor, I have to admit this, do I feel any need for it.

Yes, I have often wondered about that because some religious topics do appear in your art, for example the Ave Maria (Pl.33).

That's true, but that is often mistaken for a kind of sympathy with the Catholic religion. That's not quite right, it's really the ritual, and the physical appearance of the ritual as well, that really attracts me. I mean, I love going into a church in Italy and sitting there and just watching and looking at these tremendous baroque altarpieces and the confessional boxes – and all the kind of paraphernalia of the Catholic Church in operation. I feel a wonder and admiration for the spectacle.

I believe your family name was changed?

Well, the name actually should be 'Marrocco'. There's a very simple explanation: it is simply that my father, when he first came to Aberdeen, didn't speak English too well. When he asked the signwriter to put his name above the shop, the

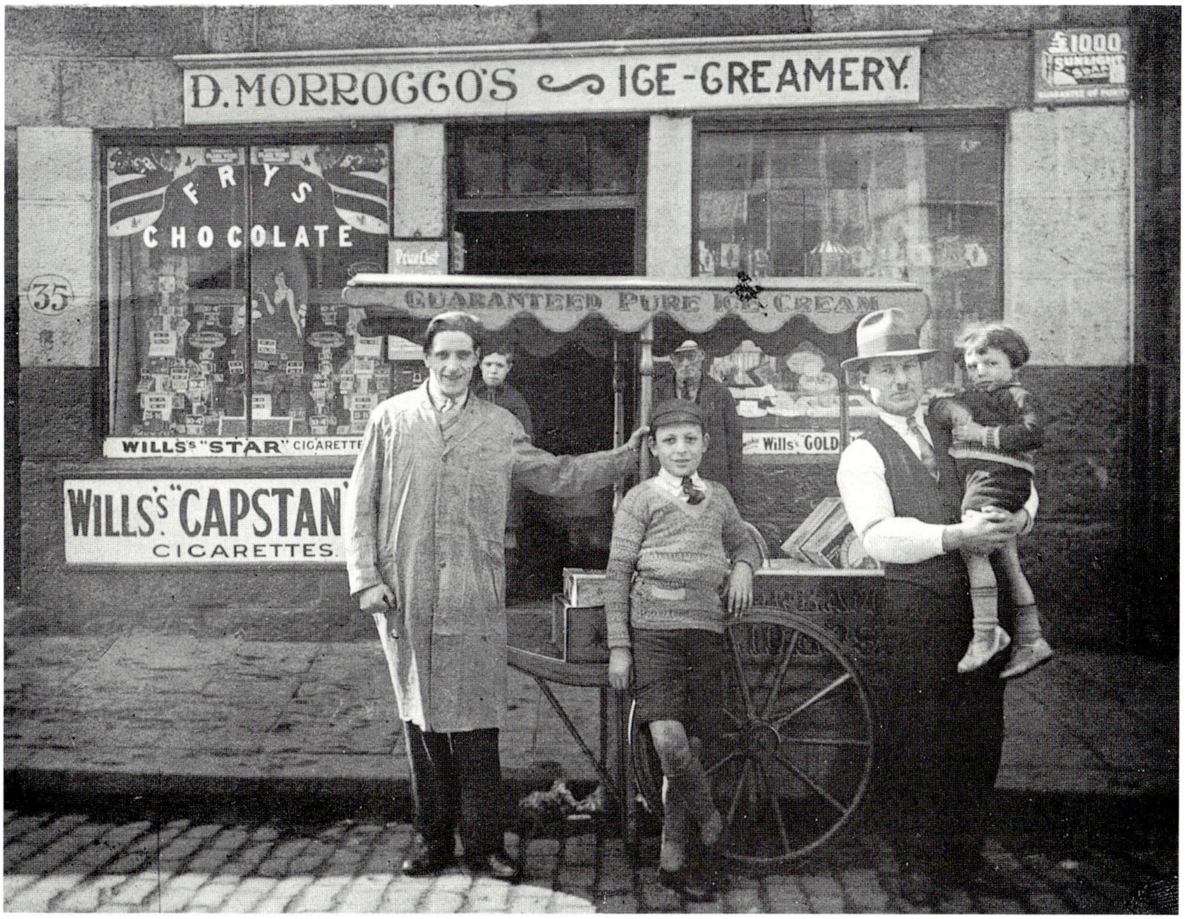

Plate 25 *Outside the Ice-Creamery, Aberdeen, c.1928. The artist is in the centre; his father and brother Val are on the right*

signwriter misspelt it and put an 'o' instead of an 'a' and my father just let it go. Well, it didn't seem to matter then, you see, for some reason. But my birth certificate is 'Marrocco' and so is his, of course. So the name is certainly not spelt correctly.

The time Val was born, was he . . . ?

No, his is still correctly spelt 'Ma' – we were brought up thinking it was 'Mo' and the first time I knew it was wrong was when I got my British passport. I was going on a scholarship at the age of nineteen or twenty and suddenly realised the name was different and the Passport Office wouldn't issue a passport – it took six months to get one. I have often thought of actually changing it back – I mean using the proper name – but it is too late because I sign everything now 'Mo' and it would look like a different person.

Another question then. Your brother Val is an architect and you are a painter. Is there any evidence of artistic talent in your forebears?

No, not as far as I know, not a vestige in any way, except – and this is only a theory – but observing my mother, she was what you might call 'artistic' in a kind of instinctive sense. She was a great person for making hats, cutting up bits of material – and making them into another kind of style. She liked the idea of the style and creating

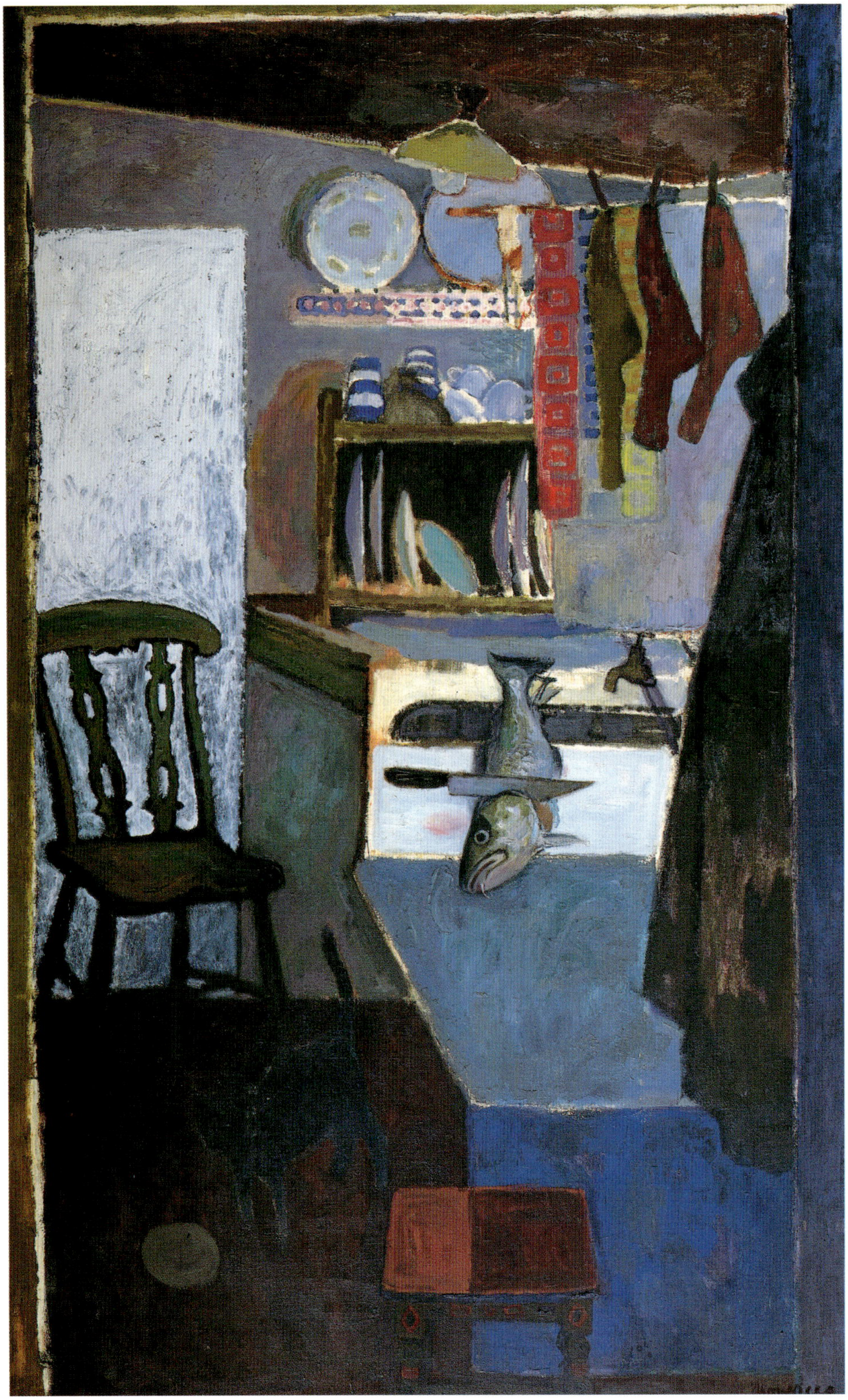

Plate 26 *Interior with a Hungry Cat*, c.1958 (Cat.46)

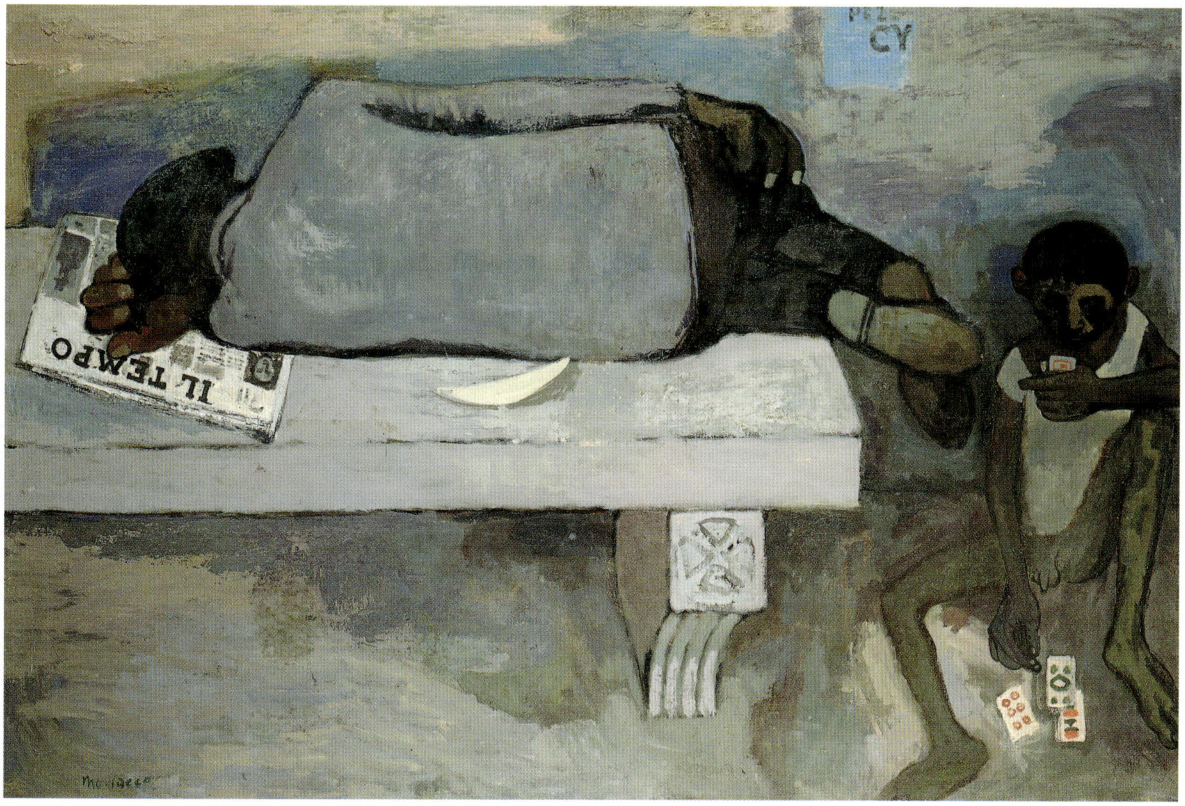

Plate 27 *I Poveri*, c.1959 (Cat.48)

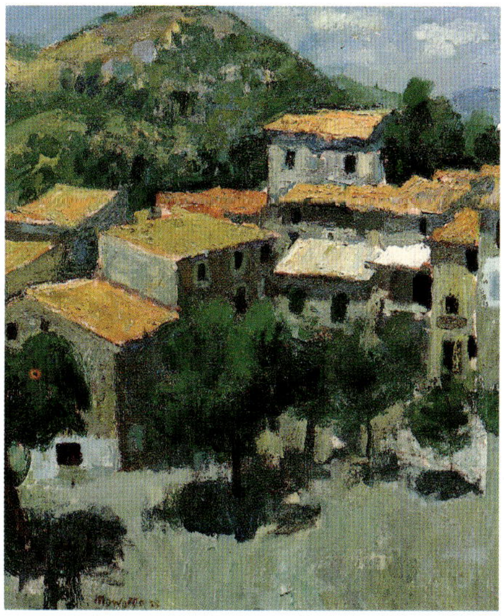

Plate 28 *Anticoli*, 1958 (Cat.45)

something different, and I think the kind of creative thing must have come from her, really.

Artistically, were you a child prodigy?

Well, I hate to use that word. I suppose I was picked up early at school – I was always the best at art in the school – and I was always a friend of the art teacher. In fact I started so early at the art college because of the art teacher I had – a Miss Green. I was going to leave the school when I was fifteen in any case because I hadn't actually had any idea of staying on, so she decided she would approach the art college. In those days the whole system was very, very loose – everyone went to the art college at roughly seventeen but if you wanted to go earlier, nobody would stop you. So I was there at fourteen and immediately sort of established myself as one of the people around who was prepared to do something – and I got a reputation of being a bit of a prodigy.

STUDENT AT GRAY'S

You went to art college when you were only fourteen – was that unusual?

Very unusual then, yes it was. Nobody else that I knew of had done it. I was always the youngest in any group that I was in – and I quite enjoyed it actually.

Your teachers at college were James Cowie and Robert Sivell. Your artistic foundation seems to have been very rigorous. Could you tell me about it?

Well, Gray's School of Art was a small art school in a neo-classical building, rather a nice building. It was attached to the art galleries, you know, with a connecting passageway – rather like the Royal College of Art connected to the V and A. I came in as a fourteen-year-old into a system of teaching which had gone on since the inception of the college in the 1860s – the painting school was based on the precepts of Velázquez. Figure painting was done on a large scale – life-size canvases of the male nude and the female nude in heroic poses with a staff maybe, sometimes older men with beards. They were all round the life rooms in the art college, these huge six-foot canvases – standard size. Very able most of them, actually first-class in the way of technical ability. There was not much emphasis on what I would call imaginative picture-making: there was a great deal of emphasis on still-life as well, and on drawing – all from the human figure. That was the kind of style – it was a kind of classical style of education that went on for my first couple of years.

Was James Cowie Head of Painting when you arrived in 1932?

No, the Head of Painting was a man called John Greig who was steeped in the style I am talking about. In 1933 or 1934 D. M. Sutherland became Principal of the art college. He came from Edinburgh, and his influence changed things. Very soon afterwards he brought in James Cowie to take over as Head of Painting. Cowie wasn't a bombastic, forceful personality – he had rather an insinuating kind of personality, quiet and intellectual. He worked by quiet persuasion and his method of teaching was simply through drawing, basically – he was a fantastic draughtsman in a kind of stylised way; you know his drawings, of course. He wasn't a free painter – he was a tight painter: his own particular idols were the early Flemish and French painters, and Quattrocento Italian painters as well, rather than the later High Renaissance stuff. He was there for nearly two years and during that time I learned to draw in that very tight, intellectual sort of way, if you like to call it that – a very analytical way. You saw some of the drawings.

Absolutely tremendous. I am so impressed with your portfolio of student drawings – they look like old master drawings.

Well, that was the sort of thing we were all trying to do. Cowie approved – that was what he was trying to do as well.

Can I just ask about Cowie's method of drawing. You have got this wonderful sort of tonal drawing – how did you get that effect? (Pl.3)

Well, tone was something he believed in. Contemporary drawing, especially in an art college, uses a minimum of tone – line or contour is probably more predominant. In Cowie's case his drawing was based on studies for his paintings – some of his drawing was miraculous. They are beautiful drawings in their own right but they also refer to the painting – you could paint from them. So he actually would construct a drawing and use a stumper, which is a rolled-up piece of paper which the Victorians used to use actually, and with powdered black chalk or red chalk he would create the tone around so that there would be a highlight on the brow – he would create a half-tone around it and then a deeper tone without using the point of the pencil but using the stumper. Then he would draw through that again with a precise line. It wasn't a free drawing – not a kind of Matisse thing with a free-line happening. It was totally under control the whole time.

Did you master that?

Well, I mean, I was very influenced by it. But, being a young student without enough knowledge to know how far to go or how much to select from what you were looking at, I went the whole hog and some of my drawings looked almost like photographs – the tone went complete. He stopped short of that, you see, because his experience and selection of the information was good enough to actually leave it as a drawing.

Now, I think you did this Self-portrait (Pl.6) *when you were seventeen and you mentioned that you were using the Van Eyck method, whatever that is.*

Yes, I did this just about the time Cowie was leaving. He put us on to that book by Max Doerner – a book on the materials and methods of the artist. I used to read this. I was always interested in how a thing is done and because of the precise Cowie method of drawing, I thought it would be a good idea to separate the colour from the drawing underpainting, as Van Eyck did. Now everybody paints *alla prima* – you put on a tone, a colour and drawing with the one stroke. But to separate the thing was what I was trying to do, so I read up the Van Eyck method – primed the canvas according to the old method by using a gesso ground, tinted the ground green, drew on it with pen and ink or with a very fine brush with a sort of raw umber. I copied it from my drawing *(Pl.2)*, I even traced it from the drawing actually and then did it in cross-hatching. I overpainted it with thin paint and gradually got thicker until I worked up to the highlights in monochrome – this was all in a kind of greenish-brown monochrome – and then started glazing it when it was dry with thin

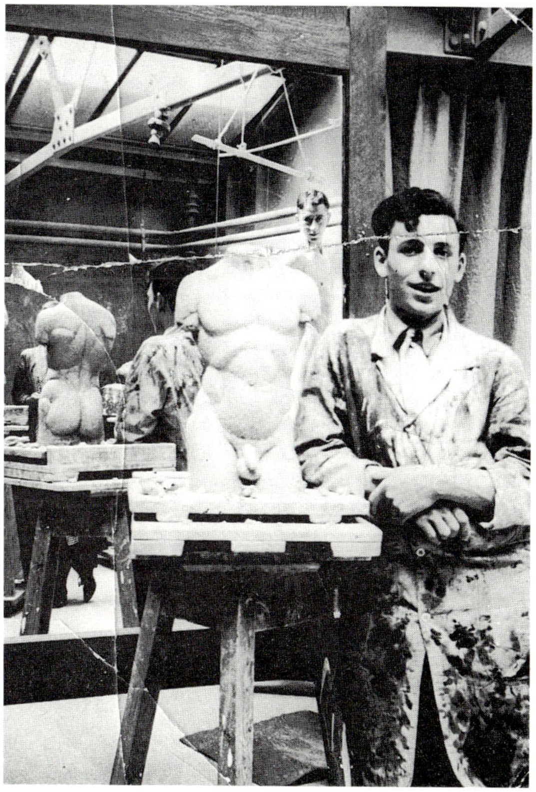

Plate 29 *Alberto Morrocco with his sculpture at Gray's School of Art*

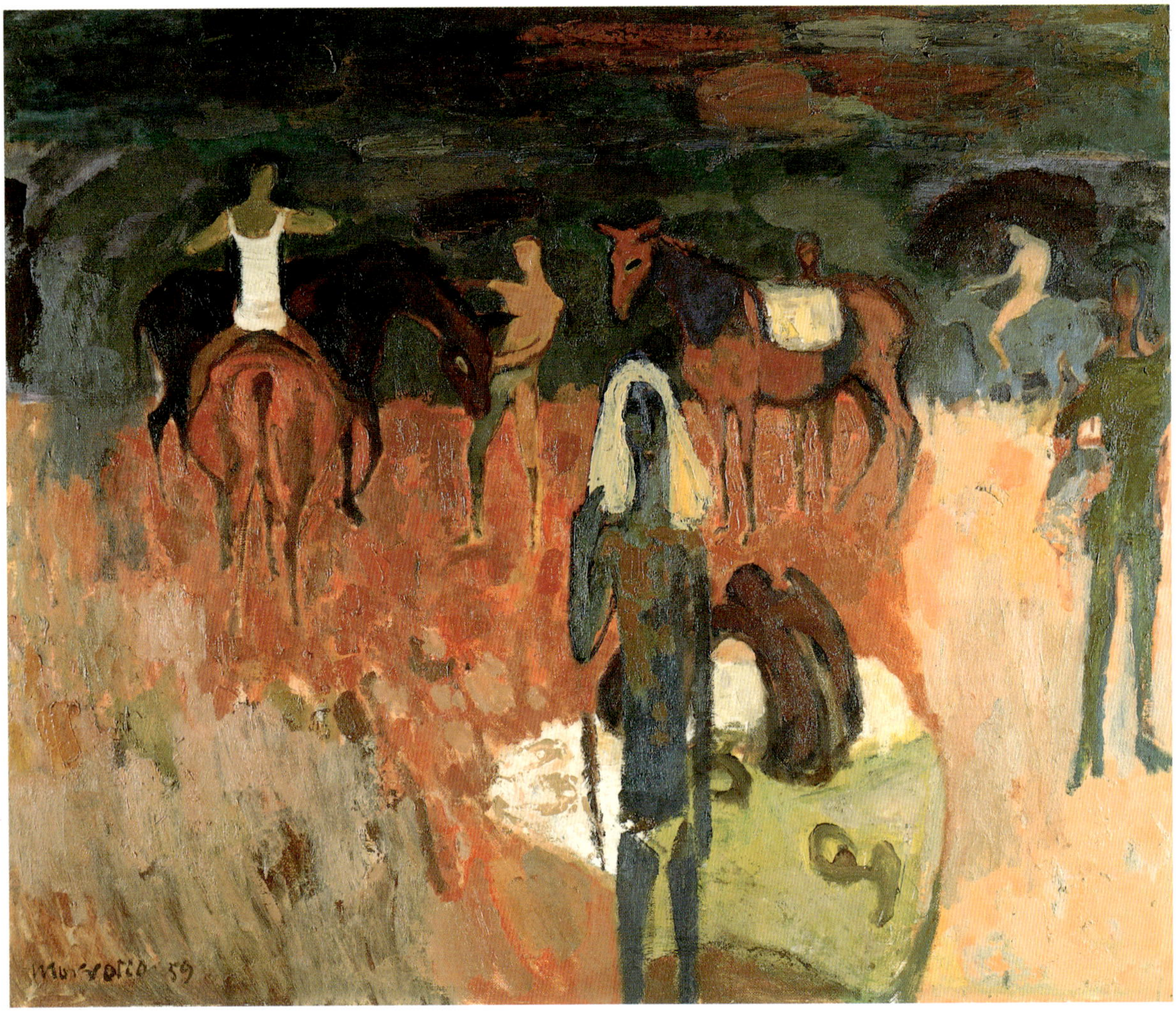

Plate 30 *Riders on a Beach*, 1959 (Cat.50)

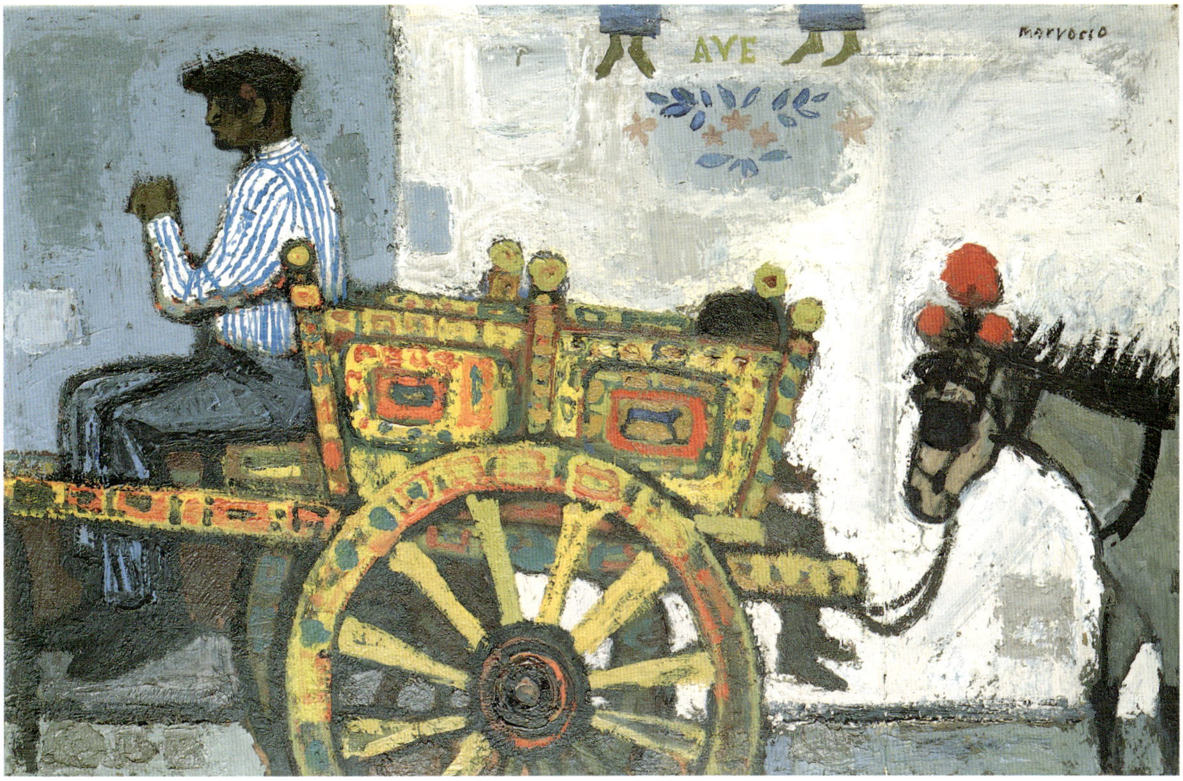

Plate 31 *Sicilian Cart*, c.1960 (Cat.52)

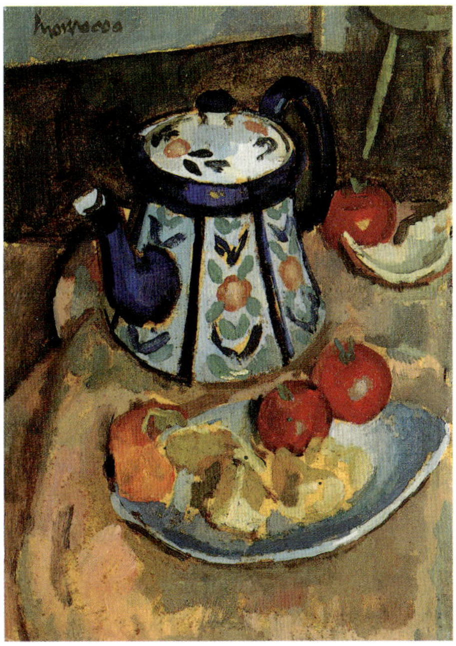

Plate 32 *The Chinese Teapot*, c.1959 (Cat.51)

glazes of pigment, pinks and whatever to get the colour values. You see that was the old master method for a long time, that's a rough translation of it.

Tell me – you mentioned this to me a while ago – at one time in the class you started painting a cubist picture.

That was earlier in my first year as a student. Right from the word go I discovered Picasso – I mean as a fourteen or fifteen-year-old I was reading about Picasso. That was unusual in those days. Picasso was known but he wasn't altogether the flavour of the month in 1932-33. I used to go up to the public library, where they had some more recent books, and see what was going on in other places, and I discovered Cubism. So I looked at all these cubist pictures in these books and there was a magazine called *Die Kunst*, a German magazine which used to show continental painters, including the French. So in the life room – we were doing life drawing – I started a series of drawings based on the kind of cubist precepts, you see. I used a piece of conté crayon – you know the square block conté crayon – and drew not with a line but with gradated area of tone round the edge of every form. One day I was in one of the life rooms with one of the female teachers who had taken the class. In came John Greig who was the Head of Painting – I was a first-year student so I was of no importance – but he came in to see how we were getting on. He saw this drawing I was doing – and it was exaggerated as well as having this odd squarish technique – and he nearly blew a fuse. 'What's this you are doing?' he said.

'I am trying to do some cubism,' I said, innocently.

And, my God, he said, 'Get up,' he said – now as a fourteen-year-old I was used to being told what to do by the teachers – so I got up, and he said, 'Get out of this studio and stand out in the corridor and I will see you in a few minutes.' So I went out and stood in the corridor – not a soul to be seen. He took his time – he went round all the class, obviously – and when he came out he gave me the most awful ripping-off for daring to do that sort of rubbish in his life room, all this Picasso stuff. I was really shattered, I must admit – I can still remember it to this day. I had to go back into the studio with my tail between my legs with the rest of the students laughing, of course. But you see, I very early on cottoned on to what was probably the aftermath of the post-impressionists. I even tried the odd abstract thing. He retired that year, this man. I wasn't allowed to do anything he was not keen on. Cross-hatching was out – you couldn't do any cross-hatching in a drawing – he hated it, you see; it had to be a rather smooth drawing, like the paintings they were doing at that time.

There was another thing you told me about with the black hearse you saw.

That was later, when D. M. Sutherland came. Now D. M. Sutherland was a gentleman of a man – he was a lovely man. Being the Principal, he had no teaching programme but I think he longed to be involved in the teaching as well, so he instituted a composition class on a Friday and he took it. He loved this – he used to come in and used to sit down with us, one student at a time, and make little sketches and go over everything. We were all struggling to understand what composition was about. There were no lectures as such. Nobody explained what composition was in painting, really, and I used to worry about it. They would tell us to look for things – look around you and use that as subject matter. One day I saw a funeral passing – some important person. It was an old-fashioned thing with black horses and with black furry plumes sticking up. I thought, my, what a great idea that would be. I had seen a reproduction of Courbet's painting of *The Funeral at Ornans*. So I did a rather free translation of this funeral with a lot of people in black mourning clothes and top hats, if you please – very severe and all black shapes. I was making sketches for it – I thought I was getting on great – and D. M. Sutherland suddenly came along and it was my turn to have a little criticism and sit down and have a chat. He didn't lose his temper – he said, 'No, I don't think so, Morrocco, I don't think so. That's rather too too sad and depressing as a subject, isn't it? No, no, I would just give that up.' So I had to give it up, you see, and I can tell you that really shattered me as well. He was a nice man – he didn't like depressing things like that.

Tell me a bit about Robert Sivell, your next tutor.

I think that Sivell is at the moment a much underrated painter, whose work is never seen – nobody talks about him. I think it's time he was revived, myself, but whether it will happen I don't know.

After Cowie left – he went to Hospitalfield – a new Head of Painting was appointed, Robert Sivell. Now Sivell was a friend of Cowie's incidentally – they were part of the same group of Glasgow students – but he was a totally different personality, quite the opposite. He was flamboyant. He was thrawn in his protestations about what you should do and what you shouldn't do and he condemned things which he didn't think were any good. You weren't allowed to have a big ego, that's for sure. If you showed the slightest signs of being vain about what you were doing, you were flattened immediately – which was not a bad thing, now when I look back on it. But his style of painting was certainly based on the Italian Renaissance – he was a great admirer of Botticelli, Leonardo, Michelangelo, Tintoretto, Titian – the lot, really. He had a wide range of interests in Italian painting. Drawing was not so important to him although he did stress it with the students, but not as much as Cowie did.

I believe Sivell's palette was very limited.

Yes, he believed in a limited palette, rather like the Italian painters themselves. It was black, white, yellow ochre, light red, terre verte, alizarine crimson, ultramarine and maybe a touch of carmine. It was a sonorous palette.

Val told me that you had quite an intense maestro-pupil relationship with Robert Sivell.

Yes, that's true. There were only five students in my year – incredible to think of it now. As a result it was a kind of student-master relationship rather based on the old atelier method that took place in Italy in the Middle Ages, and that suited Sivell – he loved that idea – he liked to feel he was the master with a group of young people following his ideas and methods.

All of us that year were influenced by Sivell because he was a powerful personality – I admired his work as well, and still do. We all tried to paint like him. The method in those days was actually to take the brush out of the student's hand, more or less, and say 'give me your brush' or something like that – and then you would stand by and he would say 'put on some more white' or 'put on some more terre verte on your palette' – then he would say 'now, I think the form is not working properly and you haven't emphasised this', and he would start painting. Maybe he would start to do a bit – but sometimes he got interested, you see, and painted right over the thing – and I have seen him paint over the work of a student who was having difficulties. He would forget all about the student and he would finish the thing. I have heard him say, 'Well, you didn't paint this, I will just take it away.' It was a valuable lesson, but one which the students often resented – I have seen students in tears. I am afraid I didn't react in that way at all – I was intrigued. He took up my portrait [*Girl in the Red Jumper*]. I wasn't in difficulties when he took it up, so I sat behind him and watched him do all this to my painting and I was intrigued with it – I wasn't resentful at all – I enjoyed it, actually.

Did they actually teach by the demonstration method?

Well, it wasn't said to be a demonstration method; he also taught just by talking as well – both ways. There were no kind of niceties about

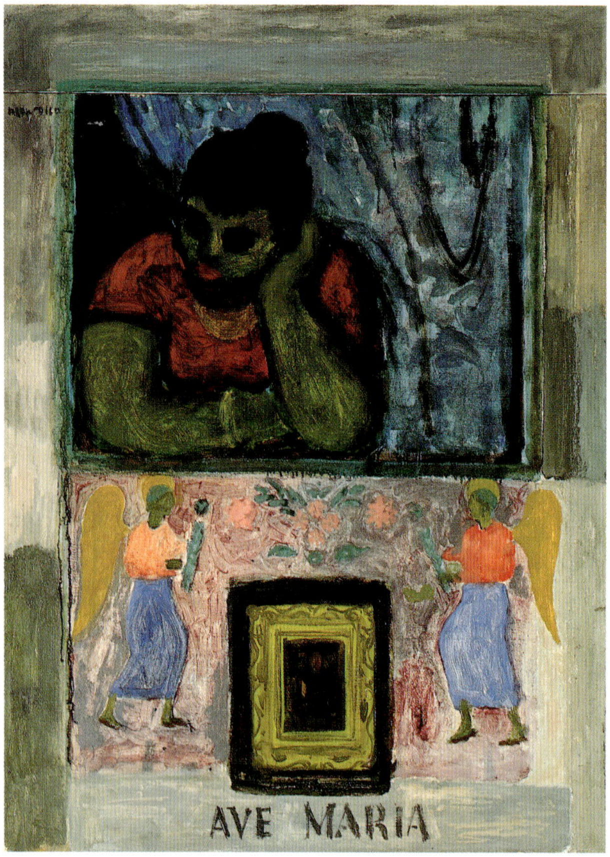

Plate 33 *Ave Maria*, c.1960 (Cat.55)

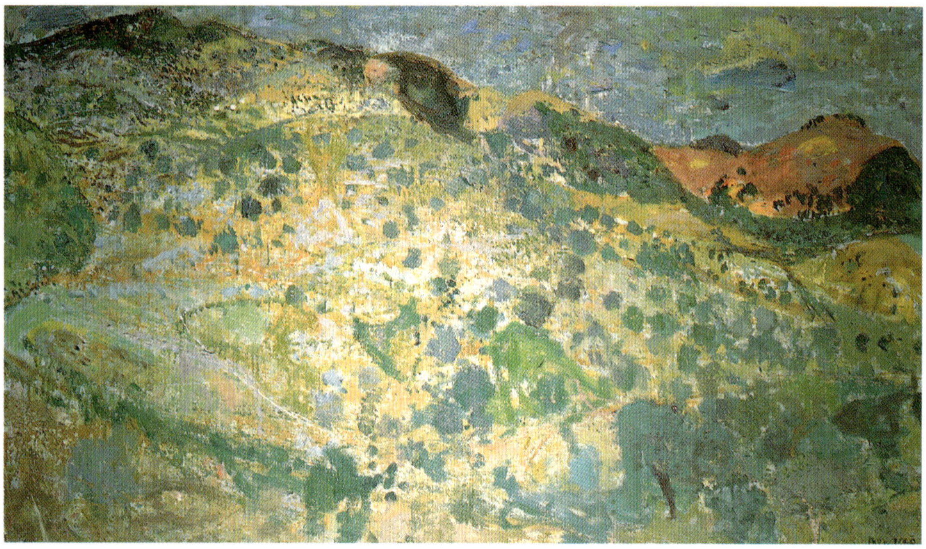

Plate 34 *Red Hill, Anticoli I*, c.1960 (Cat. 56)

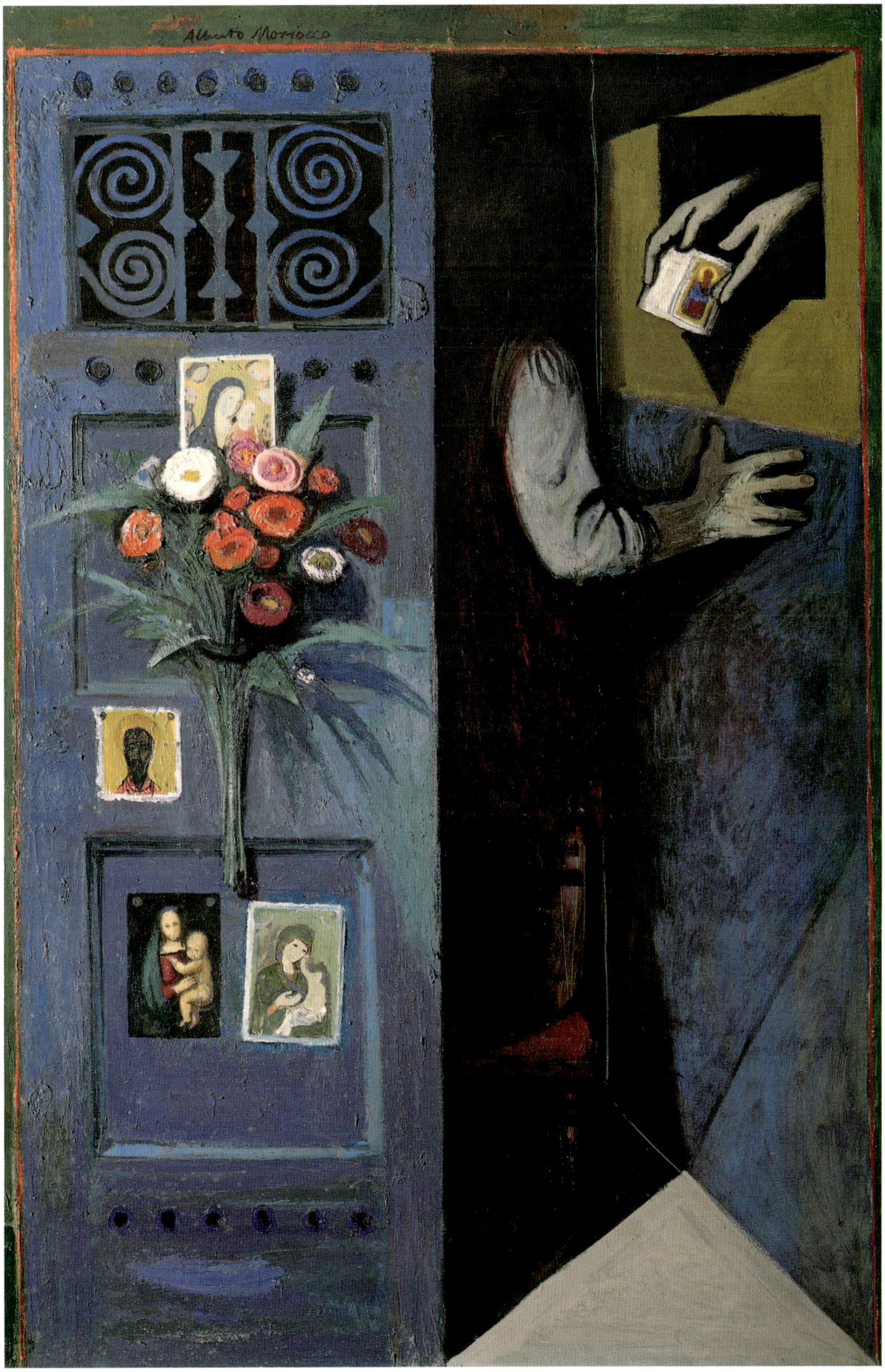

Plate 35 *Confession*, c.1962 (Cat.59)

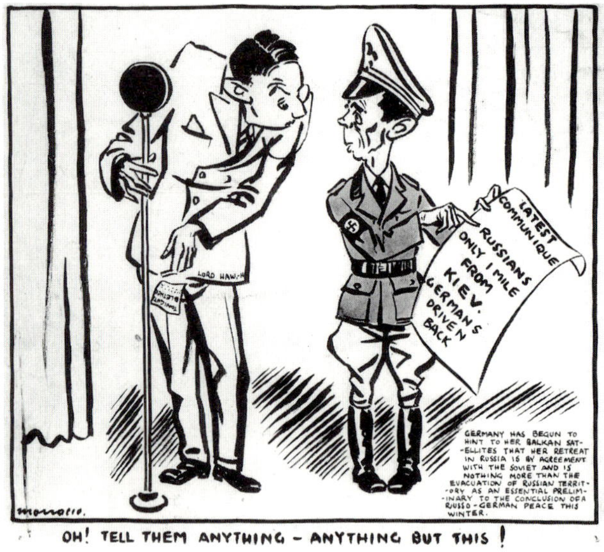

Plate 36 *Weekly wartime cartoon, Edinburgh Castle*

not touching the student's canvas – that wasn't considered important. Now it is, nobody would do that now.

The powerful Sivell influence did continue right into the 1950s. We can see it in your self-portrait of 1952. When I first saw it in Edinburgh, I was amazed by it.

To finish the art college – I had a year with Sivell, incidentally, as an assistant on the murals he was doing at Aberdeen University – the two of us were working together. I was doing all the laying-in and he was doing the finishing and so forth. So, then I was even more influenced. And then the war came – and that was six years – and then after the war I was doing a little teaching with him in the art college, so I was still under his influence, if you like. I hadn't consciously made any attempt to sort of breakthrough. I looked at the impressionists and so forth in doing things mainly out of doors, but when it came to portraits, things which he was actually influential in teaching, I was still under that kind of limited palette thing as well. That is an example of it, you see.

THE WAR

I did standard [recruit] training and then when we were stationed at Aboyne – I was in the 51st Highland Division – I was sent for by the Colonel in Charge. 'Look,' he says, 'Italy has come into the war and people who are considered dual nationals are being sent to a headquarters company. We are sending you to Edinburgh Castle.' So I was sent through to Edinburgh Castle and discovered I was among a whole lot of people who were of doubtful origin – people like the Maltese, Cypriots, Viennese and people with German origins. That was it. I had to fit into this kind of régime there. I was never sent overseas. I was in the Castle for three and a half years; I became part of the structure of the whole headquarters company.

I was employed making false wounds. They were doing training exercises all over Edinburgh, taking people off the field: they would stick a bullet wound on to the arm – it looked absolutely realistic – and so the people would come and look at it and put on the appropriate bandage for the wound. I was making these wounds for, by God, it must have been a couple of years. Then I went on to painting helmets, painting numbers and badges on helmets and things – I was in QO stores, various things like that. In the army you had to do anything. I was in a concert party. I had the most peculiar army career, I can tell you. They ran a concert party from the headquarters company and there were a lot of professional people – jazz musicians, singers – Nicky Kidd was one that I remember, a Glasgow boy. There was a comedian and jugglers, and I was a quick-sketch artist doing caricatures on the stage. We did some huge concerts in Edinburgh.

So you developed your patter?

No, it was a totally silent act. It was done with a musical background and no actual talk. There were caricatures of people like Churchill and so forth, finishing off with – which was really difficult, which was genuine – asking people from the audience to come up on stage – WAAFS or soldiers – and doing a caricature on the stage of somebody you had never seen before. *That* I can tell you was really difficult. I enjoyed all that because it's a kind of show-off thing that I always liked. One night we were doing a huge concert at one of the big cinemas and back-stage there came a gentleman, a very tall portly gentleman who had asked to see me. He came up and says, 'My name is Bond Rowell' – no, you won't know but he was the straight man with a famous Scotch comedian, Will Fyffe. 'By watching your act,' he says, 'I would like you to come on tour with us as one of the turns.' I says, 'I'm in the army,' I says, 'how can I do that?'.

He says, 'I'll see your commanding officer and see if I can arrange it.' And so he saw the commanding officer and the commanding officer sent for me. He says, 'Morrocco, I'm sorry I can't let you go – we need every man we've got in this unit.' I was a postman at the time, incidentally – so I wasn't allowed to go. But they were trying to make me a career as a music-hall artist – incredible really.

[After the war Alberto, now married to Vera Mercer and with his first son, moved back to Aberdeen. His main source of income was from teaching one and a half days a week at Gray's School of Art and a shared commission to illustrate Professor Lockhart's *Anatomy*, working from actual cadavers in the so-called 'drain' under the main tower of the University. In 1950 he became a full-time Lecturer at Gray's.]

HEAD OF ART AT DUNDEE

Now in 1950 you became Head of Painting at Dundee School of Art as it was then called. Was the job advertised?

Yes, I came down and was interviewed by Francis Cooper and the whole of the Governing Body of the School of Art and the College of Technology, then twenty-five people. It was quite a gruelling kind of interview. I could see as things went on they were fairly well disposed to me but I was unfavourably disposed to the art college, having seen it in detail. They showed me all round the place and I thought '*My God*, I don't want to come to this place.' It was a tech, you see, and the equipment was terrible, the atmosphere was awful, it was out of date; I thought, I don't want to come here.

They told you presumably about the brand new building in Perth Road?

Yes, I was told all about that but that didn't interest me at the time – it was the building as it was. And then there was Francis Cooper himself, you see – he was a Dickensian character, Francis. Anyway, they told me I had got the job and I went back to Aberdeen and I was so depressed that I sat down and wrote a letter of resignation: I am sorry but I cannot take the job – that was the finish – I will carry on in Aberdeen and settle down there. The Chairman of the Board of Governors himself came up – he spent the whole day convincing me that I was doing the wrong thing, that I should come down and eventually

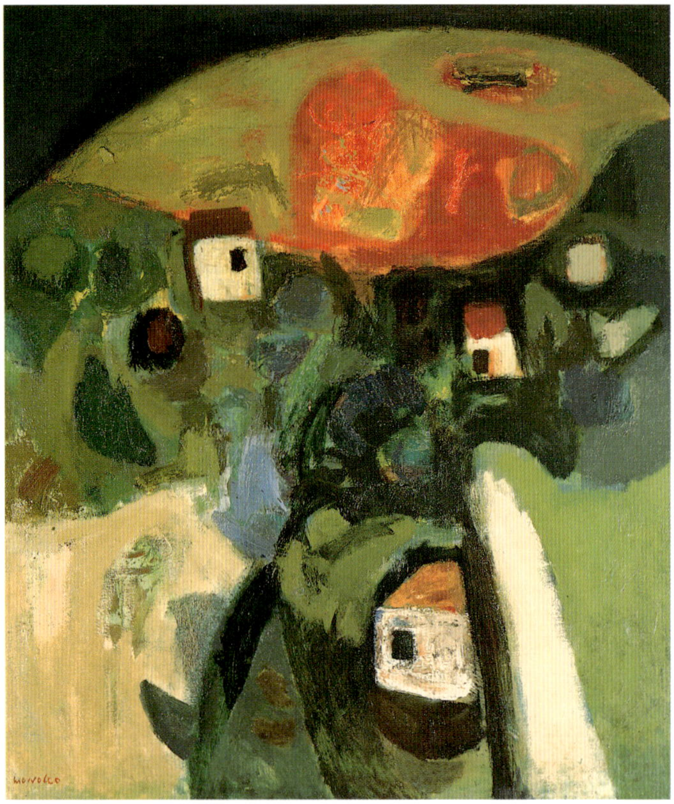

Plate 37 *Red Hill, Anticoli II*, c.1962 (Cat.64)

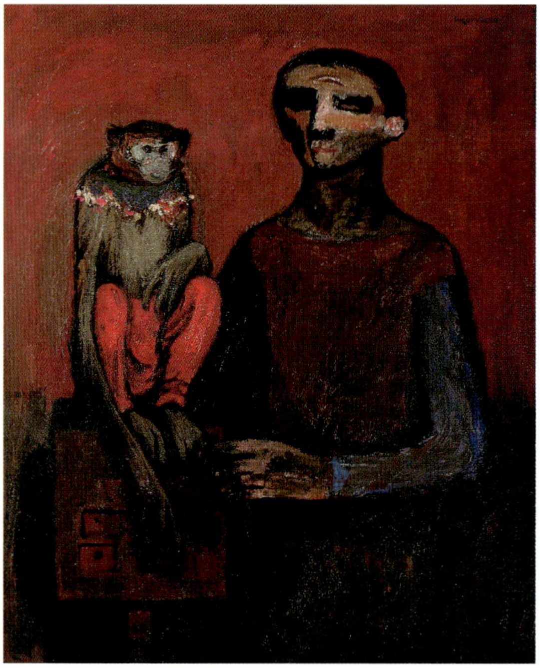

Plate 38 *Blind Fortune-teller*, c.1962 (Cat.65)

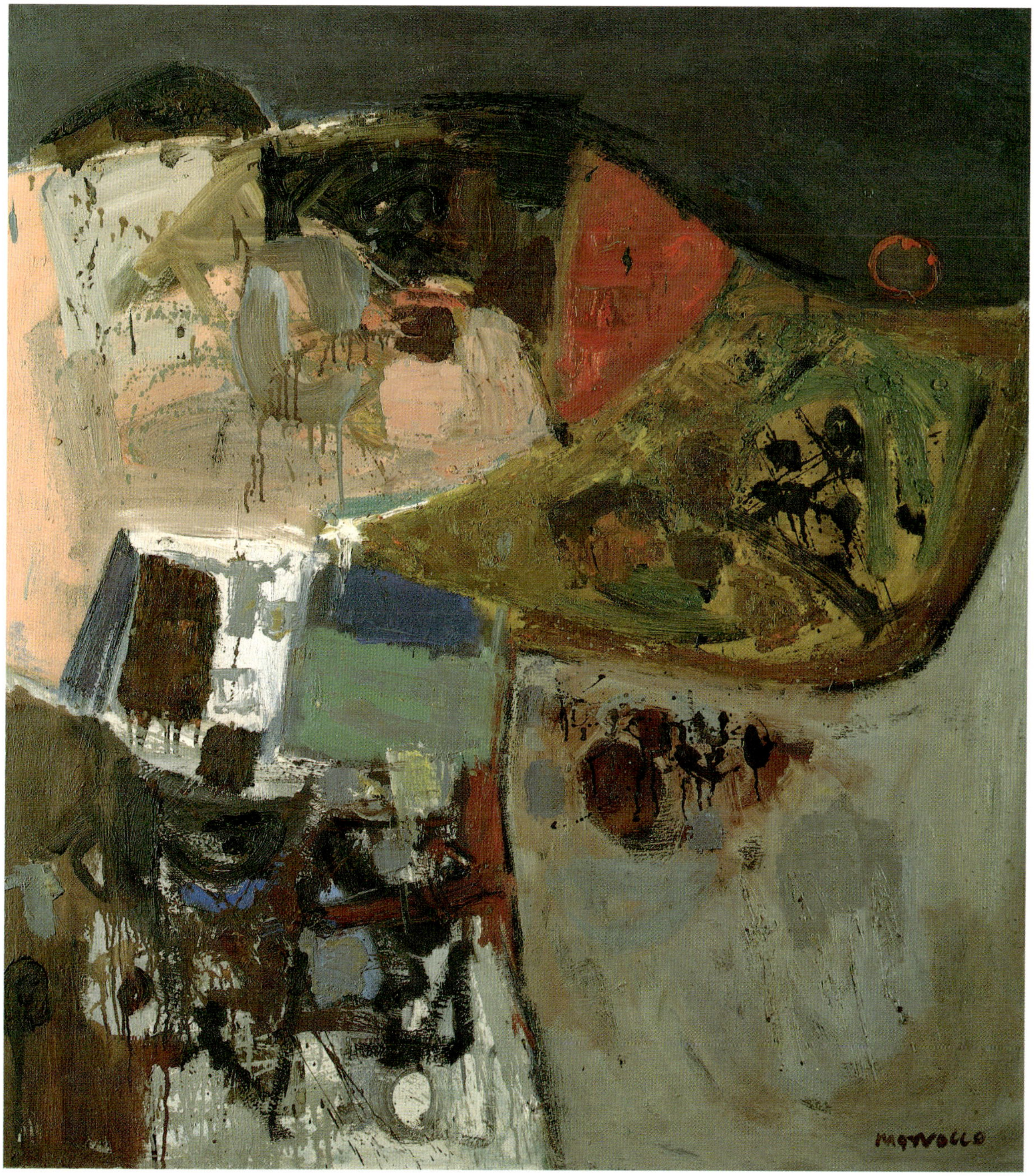

Plate 39 *Setting Sun II*, c.1962 (Cat.63)

he succeeded, you see – that's how I came to Dundee.

I hope you are glad you came.

Oh yes, I mean, as it turned out – certainly the first few years weren't very pleasant, I must admit – but at the same time once the new college was built the whole thing changed totally. It made a tremendous difference.

What was your method of teaching? What you are famous for, of course, is doing demonstrations.

Well, I didn't do any demonstrations then in the art college – I didn't attempt anything like that. When I came to the art college it was really run down – I have to say that – it was really working at half-cock. The painting students didn't know where they were going. When I arrived and saw the state of things, I was horrified: the set-ups, the lack of interest in the things they were painting and the fact that nobody had tried to tell them a method – they were all working just off the cuff themselves. I remember the very first day I went into one of the life rooms. The students had obviously been talking about me – 'We'll see what this chap can do'. I started criticising this painting. The student said, 'Can you show me?' So I said, 'Sure, right, give me your brushes.' He had the most awful brushes and palette – his equipment was just awful. Anyway, I bit on the bullet and took up his brushes and painted the head or whatever – and I think that impressed them – I think they thought, 'God, this bloke maybe can do something after all'. I carried on with roughly the same method as Sivell had done – but not as much, I didn't paint all over the canvases – but the students were so keen to actually be shown because they had had no direction given, that they were asking for me to do it and I did it. I have seen me go round the whole class one after the other, doing a bit on each one. It was hard work.

Who else was teaching painting?

There was only Jimmy Duff on the full-time staff. The rest were all part-time people, like the McKenzie sisters – they were very good at teaching. The next year I asked for an assistant lecturer – Jimmy Duff was dealing with the first year and I wanted somebody to help in the upper years – so we advertised and Gordon Cameron got the job. He was terrific, one of the strongest elements in the teaching staff. I was grateful for him coming – it would have been pretty tough going. David McClure came in 1957 and then we got various other people like Jack Knox and Peter Collins; then we got one or two ex-students that we'd trained like Dennis Buchan, Ian Fearn and Dick Hunter. The whole thing grew. By the 1960s the thing was going extremely well.

My sister went to the art college in 1968 and she remembers you doing painting demonstrations.

Round about that time I started doing one or two again. You know, the oddest thing is that I had been doing these things off and on for the Arts Council (but not in the college), going to packed audiences of amateur painters, mainly for art societies. But doing it in front of students I was always as nervous as anything because I didn't know how they would react to being demonstrated to. A lot of students didn't want to be involved in even watching, but I did one or two quite good ones actually; latterly I think the students quite enjoyed it. I didn't force that on them at all. I was never actually one to force students to do anything.

I think a lot of students obviously would be influenced by you.

Yes, especially painting in the life room – we did quite a lot of that. Painting a nude is very, very difficult for anybody – it's so subtle, you know, in front of something when you can compare what you are putting on with what you were looking at. Demonstrating what you are translating from what you saw – that is valuable to any student, I think.

TALKING ABOUT PAINTING

I believe one of the key points in your development was when you started to feel quite strongly about the search for colour.

Yes, I mean I have always been interested in colour – always – but I wasn't really interested in it as a main part of the painting. I always thought of colour as being part of the painting in relation to the form. But there comes a point when you get the form and the colour in competition – in other words, of equal importance. Then a certain vulgarity occurs because a full form with colour can be very vulgar – I began to be aware by looking at people like, say, Matisse, that you've got to let something go if something else is to predominate. If you are interested in colour, you want to get the full powerful value of it – you have got to let the *form* be less important. That is what happened to me. I even started painting things in a frontal light which doesn't have any strong cast shadow – so you were getting full value for any colour that was on the subject.

One of the things that really put me over on the side of intense colour was our visit to Tunisia some years ago now. In the marketplaces there I used to see Berber women coming in from the country and they were dressed in the most amazing collection – I remember it – of pieces of coloured draperies: hangings, scarves and blouses of colour which you might have thought would have been discordant but, because the skin was so dark, you could actually put the most powerful and intense colour against a dark skin. If you put it against a white or a pale skin it would jar. It's rather like putting a black line between two colours which are of equal pitch – the black line actually makes it work. Take away the black line, and they will hit each other. I think that same thing happens with colour in relation to human beings. So I started to use colour, trying to push it to the absolute limit of intensity within its range. That painting you have [*Still Life on Red Cloth (Pl.1)*], you see, was one of these. Using a variety of reds, with blue in some and with orange in the other – but all reds – red base – acting on each other with both a harmony and a discord.

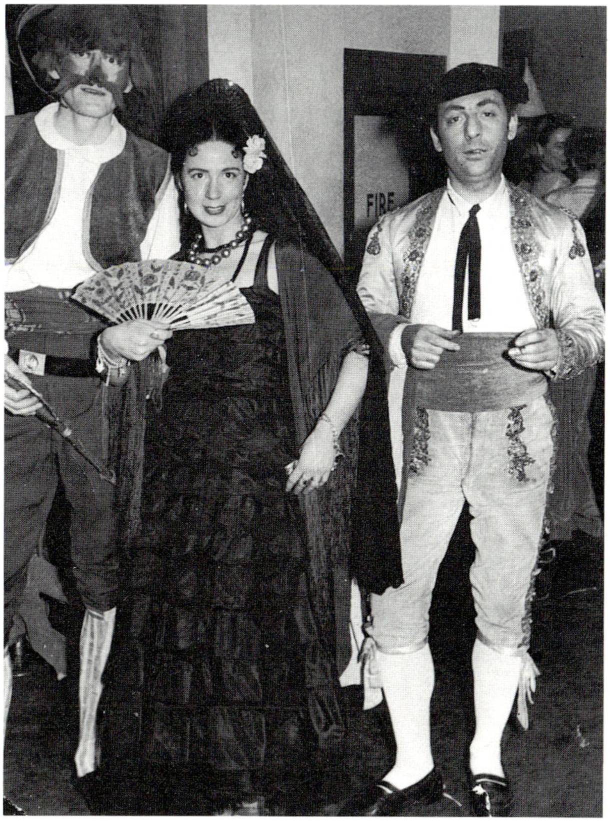

Plate 40 *The Revels at Duncan of Jordanstone College of Art (with Vera)*

That's right. But from what you say, you sacrificed the drawing, the reality and so on.

Yes, flattening the form, really.

In fact, you do deliberate distortions.

That's right, well now I do – yes. But gradually as I went on . . . when you use the same themes you tend to form a kind of type. I naturally have evolved a type which is heavy built – a female form which is fulsome – and the reason for that is not simply because you see them all the time abroad, but because they fill the space: you get a fulsome coloured shape of a certain bulk on the canvas – it actually gives a lot to work with.

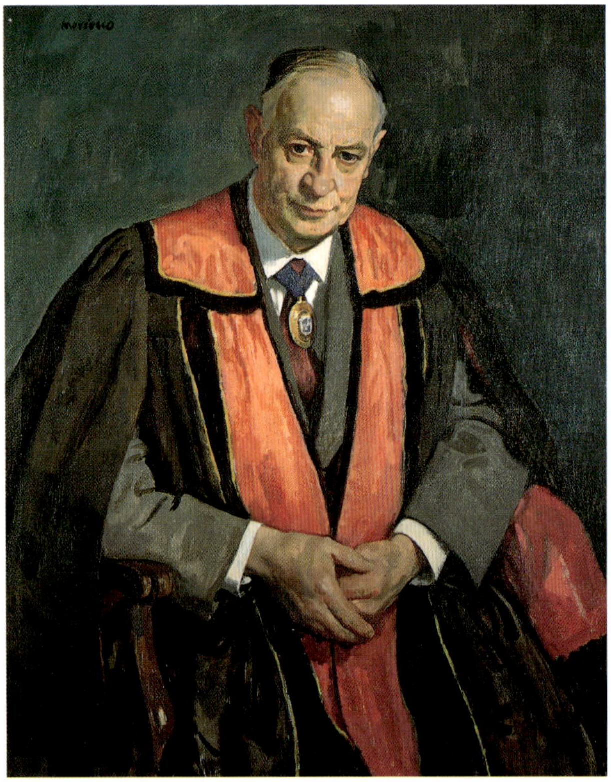

Plate 41 *Joseph H. Wright*, c.1962 (Cat.68)

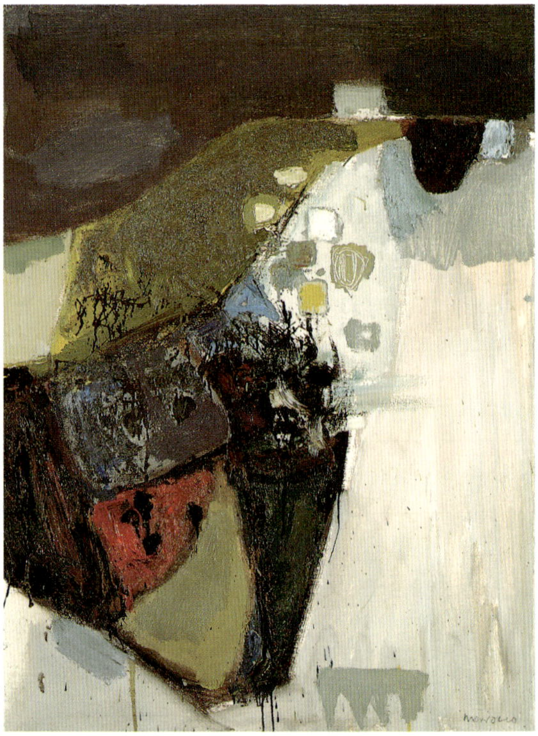

Plate 42 *Hill Village and Monastery*, c.1963 (Cat.67)

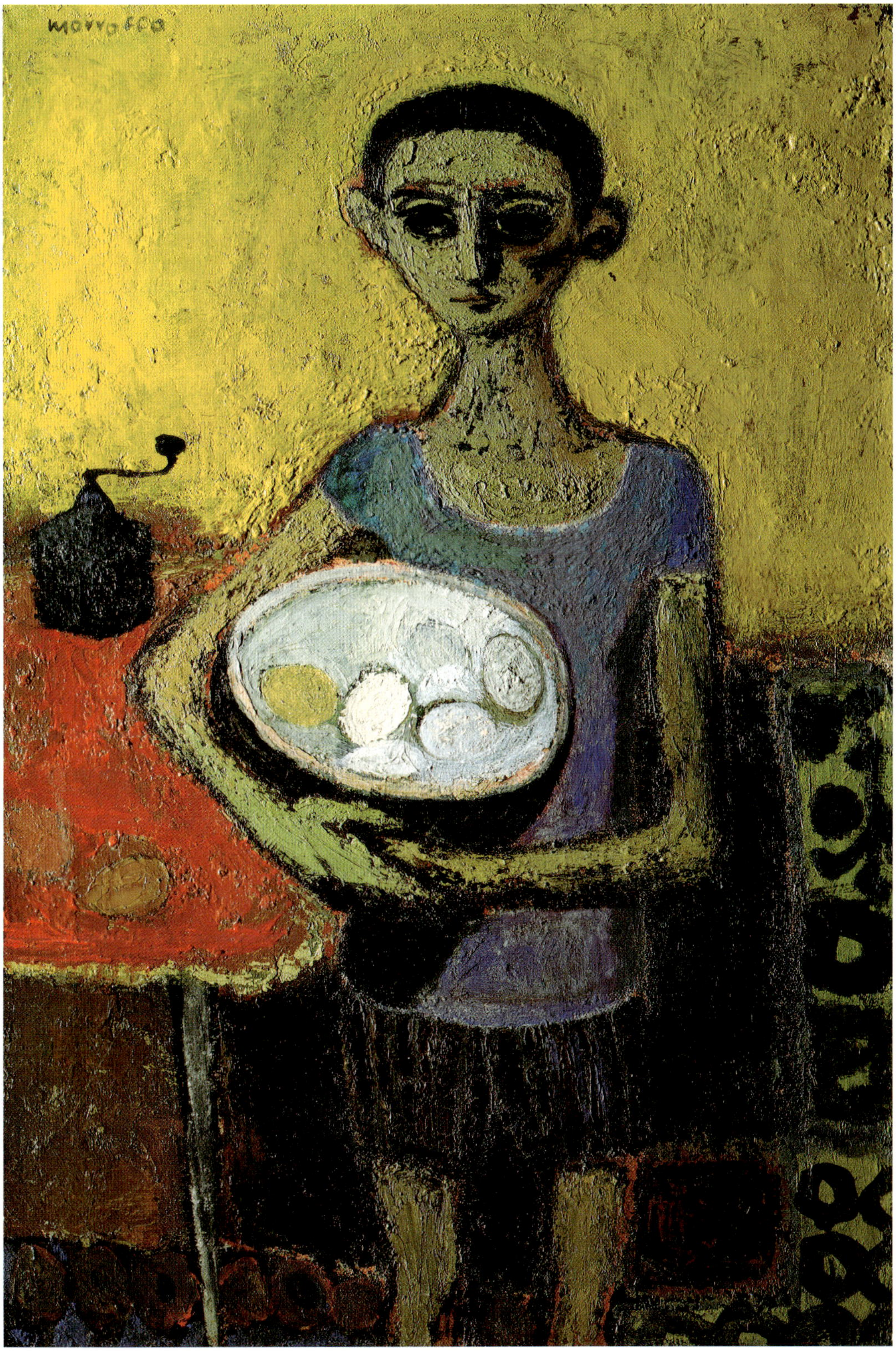

Plate 43 *Boy with Bowl of Eggs*, c.1962 (Cat.66)

But this distorted drawing, what does it owe to Matisse and Picasso?

Well, for the same reason that they . . . Picasso makes things heavy – he makes hands big and he makes legs thick. I started to see this in actual reality in peasant women in Italy. My mother was built like that a little bit. Every so often I have noticed in the figures that there is a kind of echo of my mother. So it's a mixture of two things – it is a mixture of an aesthetic use of a bulky shape as well as actually being a sympathetic female form. I find it more difficult to work with a thin form for one thing – a thin figure.

When did you start going back to Italy?

The first visit since I had been a boy was 1950. I was there when I was four or five years old, with a great gap between. I would have been there in 1939, of course, if it had not been for the war. We started going regularly after that. We used to go to this village, Anticoli, nearly every year and rent a studio.

You said this picture, I Poveri (Pl.27) *was a turning point in your career: 'This is my attempt at social realism.'*

Yes, well it is in a sense. I saw something like it – not that composition but I did do a drawing of a derelict in Palermo – a man lying on a bench, he was lying sleeping. He had been drinking, I think – there was a bottle of wine near him – and he was obviously poverty-stricken, obviously down on his luck. When I saw it, it seemed to me at that time to typify what was happening in Sicily – this was the early 1950s I am talking about. Sicily was a very poor country then, and I wanted to make some sort of comment about that as well. You used to see children like [those in *I Poveri*] in the poor quarters of Palermo and Naples with hardly a thing to wear during the summer. I put the whole thing together to make this, I suppose, a kind of social realist picture. But it is not totally so: I was actually trying to get a slightly poetic feeling, I think. It is a kind of realism, but I have always stopped short of total ugliness – I have never been able to swallow on that. A slightly classical thing comes through – it is part of my nature, I think.

[Second Interview, 24 March 1993]

Alberto, looking at the body of work you've produced in the last sixty years, one is very struck by the variety of subject matter. You've painted portraits, landscapes, townscapes, interiors, still-lifes, fantasy paintings and a wide variety of figurative paintings. Is there anything you haven't painted?

Well, I have covered most of what you might call the normal subject matter of painting throughout the past four or five hundred years. I haven't painted any complete abstracts. I have dithered on the edge of abstraction once or twice because I regard the abstract idiom as quite important, in fact, to all kinds of paintings. It isolates an important factor in any kind of painting whether it be realism or expressionism or whatever. But I find when I go into total abstraction I lose the place – I lose the point in fact – so I haven't gone in that direction. I have to start with something either seen or felt or both at the same time before I can see a picture – an expression of some idea.

Yes. I've often thought that there were a lot of abstract qualities in your work – often very strong in the composition, the geometry and the use of colour and tone. I mean, that's what I personally look for in paintings. I just see that you're going that way – but using as a start the figurative material.

As I say, I don't think I could ever go completely abstract.

Which artists do you most admire – past and present?

Past and present? One has to take the old masters in the great tradition. I admire Velázquez very much because of his complete control both in technique and in the organisation of the idea and his cool observation – standing back a little from the subject. He is almost the opposite of an expressionist painter. That doesn't mean to say that there's not an emotive idea behind the thing. *Las Meninas* is a masterpiece by any standards. One of the great painters of the last four or five hundred years.

Now an artist of a different kind but who is nevertheless connected is Titian, whose technique uses a rich kind of impasto. But he is not a cool painter in the sense that Velázquez was. He does become involved – he does become a little expressionist in the modern sense of the word – and he is a great colourist, of course.

How about the modern people – anybody in this generation?

I am a tremendous admirer of Picasso, of course – who isn't? But Picasso has said everything actually, and he's said it in so many languages – that's the other thing. I mean, he is the great exponent of style, there's no question about it. Also he never bores: that's one of his great virtues. Some artists can be extremely able but they can be a little dry, a little tedious occasionally. Picasso never is. Even his worst painting is full of some kind of animal interest, if you like. He is without doubt a genius. He's tried everthing – any idea that's crossed his mind, he's had a shot at it. He hasn't drawn back and said 'No, I can't do that, it's not my style': he's just done it anyway – and that takes a bit of courage as well.

A painter like Matisse I greatly admire as well and in some ways he's a greater *painter* than Picasso. He's concerned, I think, more with the traditional use of paint as a medium. I mean, he actually cherishes the quality of the paint a bit more than Picasso – Picasso simply makes the paint do what he wants it to do, whether it likes it or not. But Matisse has a gentler, more humane approach and I react strongly to that as well. And, of course, he's another great colourist.

Can we look at your portraits now? For over thirty years, until the mid-1980s, you painted about five or six commissioned portraits a year.

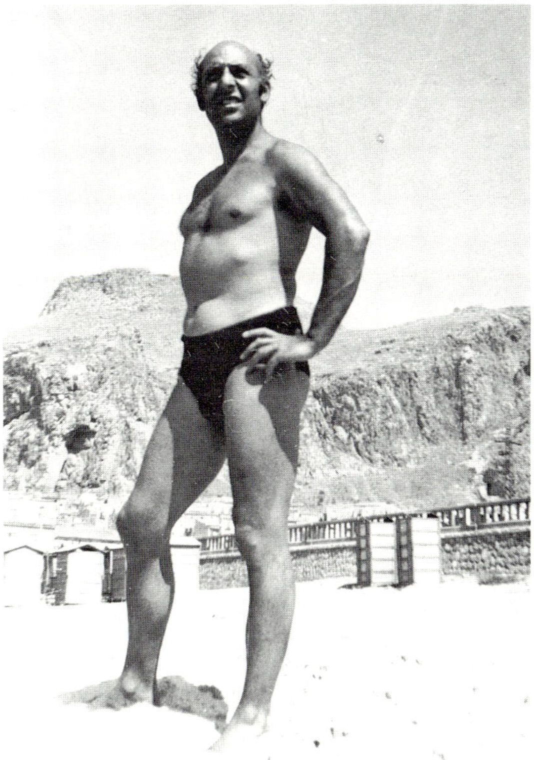

Plate 44 *On a beach in Sicily*

In fact, you're still in great demand. You also do self-portraits and portraits of the family. What makes for a successful portrait in your view?

A variety of things, actually. But, I take the view – which is probably considered a little old-fashioned nowadays – that a portrait has to satisfy two main things. One is, and this is very important, that it should act in the same way as any other painting – it should give off a sense of immediate pleasure in the way it has been handled, and the way the composition and the colour have been organised – quite apart from the subject. But, at the same time, it's got a specific intention and that is to depict another human being. Now, there's a variety of opinions about how this should be done. Whether one paints in a purely objective way or whether one paints in a more abstract way or even in an expressionist way, the brief is that you must

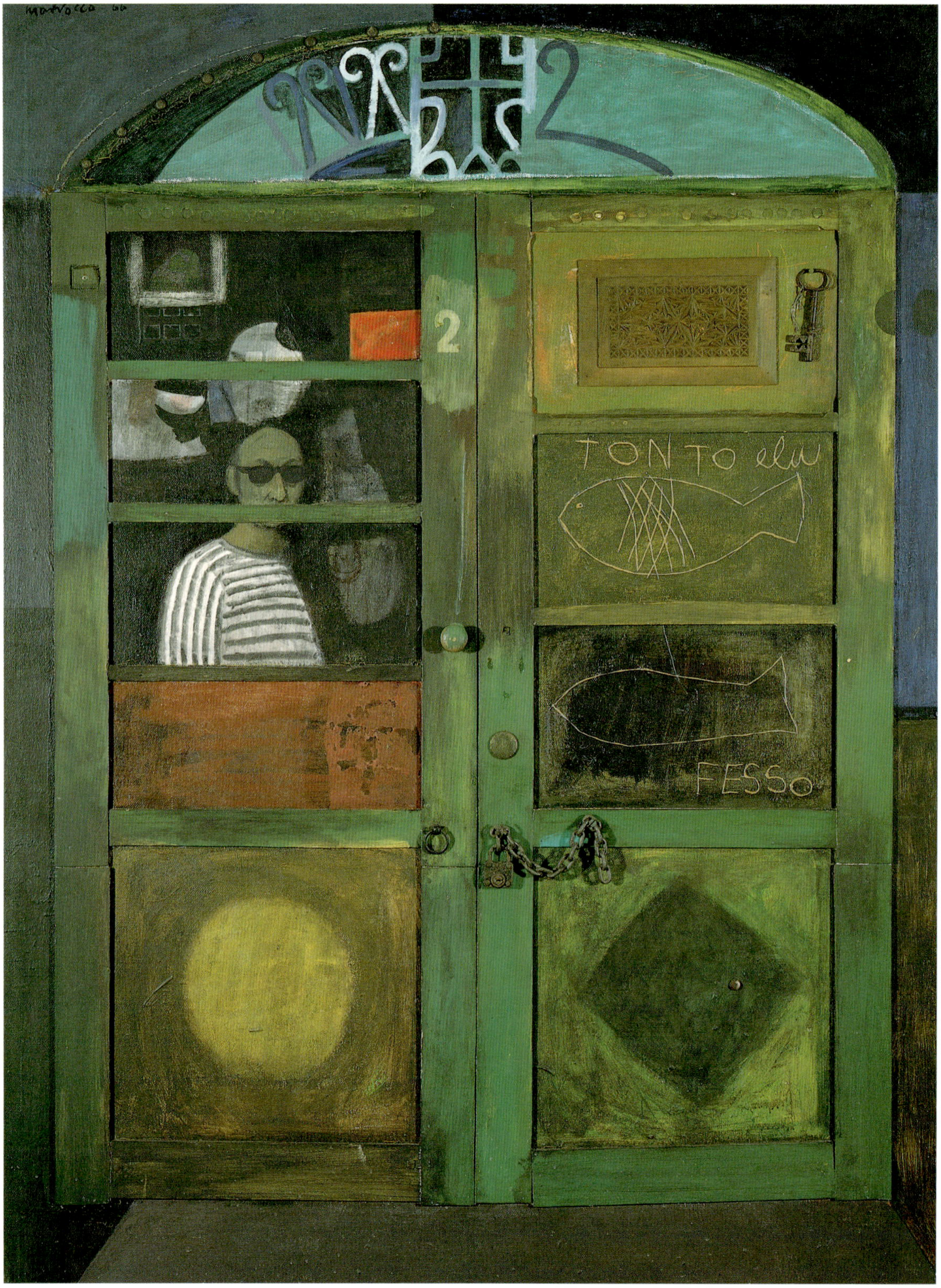

Plate 45 *Door in Orbitello*, 1966 (Cat.73)

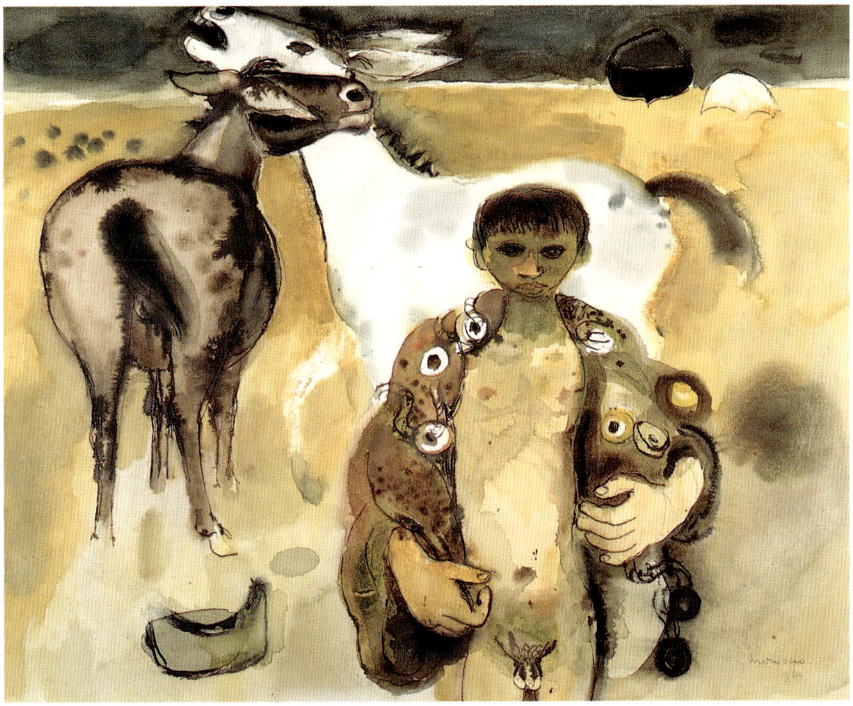

Plate 46 *Watering the Donkeys, Cefalu*, 1966 (Cat.76)

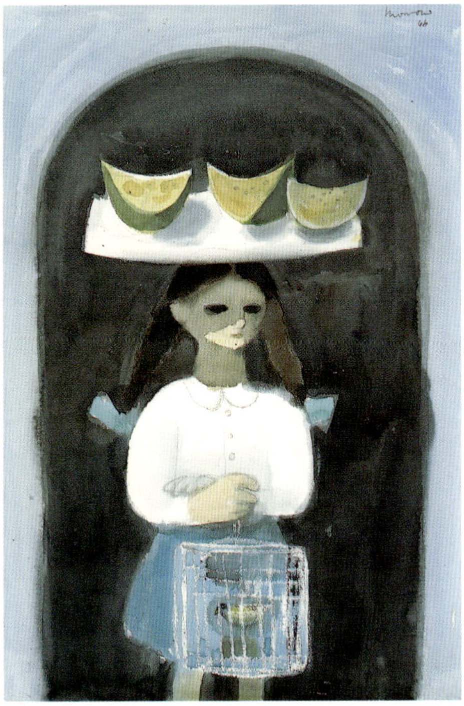

Plate 47 *Girl with Melons*, 1966 (Cat.74)

make a physical likeness. I use the word 'physical' deliberately: not simply a psychic likeness or a vague spiritual likeness, but a *physical* likeness first. The other things can be involved in that physical likeness but it must satisfy that first of all – otherwise it really isn't a portrait. Again I must come back to Velázquez, a great portrait painter. The portrait of his daughter in the Wallace Collection in London is a masterpiece; his portrait of Juan Pareja, his mulatto studio assistant who posed for him as a sort of pre-runover before he painted the Pope Julius VI portrait, is another great masterpiece. These are complete – you don't *have* to know that these were likenesses – one doesn't know; but I am totally convinced – I mean, I know by the way the thing's painted – that these were what one may call spitting likenesses – quite apart from having all the other virtues I have spoken of before.

What about the sitter's personality?

Again, I have often been asked 'how do you express the personality of the sitter?'. The answer is very simple: by reacting to the personality of the sitter. Now, there's no recipe for that – you can't say, 'well this man has got bushy eyebrows, therefore I'll exaggerate that and that will express some part of his character'. I don't believe that's the way it works. It's an instinctive thing. It's one human being reacting to another. It's like people in conversation with each other – you form opinions while you are talking to somebody.

Do you need to feel a rapport with the sitter?

Yes, I think you need to have some kind of rapport. If you are actually faced with the problem of painting somebody whom you totally dislike it may lead to a kind of grotesque caricaturist type of painting, which may express your feelings and may well be a fine portrait too – that's possible. The worst kind of reaction I think is no reaction – in other words, if you're faced with somebody who's got a boring personality and a bland physical appearance, that's very difficult.

Do you flatter your sitters?

I try not to. That's one of the crucial points about portrait painting. Flattery is a difficult word to define – there is a kind of limit when it goes over the top. If you are actually quite consciously and deliberately flattering so that the person will like the portrait and pay you a handsome fee without any argument, I think that's dishonest, totally dishonest. But I can look at a painting by, say, Van Dyke: now Van Dyke was a great portrait painter – elegant, beautifully painted – but you never see anybody with baggy eyes or dewlaps or wrinkles in a Van Dyke. Everything is smoothly, beautifully elegant. That's verging on the edge of flattery – but it isn't flattery of the kind I was talking about before – it's being kind to the sitter, really.

How did you get on with Lord Cameron? (Pl.65)

Extremely well because I already knew him quite well before we started the portrait. I was very flattered when he asked me to paint it. He is a distinguished man – and looks a distinguished man, that's the other thing. He is almost a kind of Raeburn character and the oddest thing is at the time I painted his portrait I had the use of the Raeburn Studio in Edinburgh. The fact that I was painting in Raeburn's old stamping ground with somebody who could have been painted by Raeburn in a sense – I think it influenced me slightly. And the top lighting in the studio – Raeburn had a series of shutters put on the windows to get all kinds of dramatic lighting – I used that a little bit more than I would normally have done. The sittings were very good – we talked quite a lot and so forth. I tried to use the red robe – the university robe – without actually putting it on, without making it too formal a portrait, by slinging it over the back of the chair. And the use of a very dark background with his black jacket, and the red, and the yellow waistcoat which is a keynote in the colour scheme, gave the thing a kind of power. I regard that as one of the best portraits I have ever done.

Let us turn to your landscape paintings. In organising the exhibition we have been most interested in a group of semi-abstract landscapes you did in the early 1960s, such as Red Hill, Anticoli I (Pl.34). *How do you feel about them now?*

Well, I regard some of these as being quite powerful. That was the period when the action painting movement was taking place in America. I used to look at these things by Jackson Pollock and various other people and there was a kind of vivacity about them. You know the style of painting – the paint was loosely applied, applied almost accidentally . . . it rather influenced me at the time. I was in Italy painting in this little village and I began to see the landscape – a very broken sort of spotty landscape around that region with great mounds of rock – in terms of that style. As a result of that I began to put the paint on with a kind of a flick, actually using liquid paint almost – I used to carry it in tins – and start the painting off by flinging a lot of paint on the canvas so that I could then work through that and get the effect I was looking for in the landscape. These were all done on the spot, actually. *Red Hill, Anticoli* – that's about a five-foot canvas – I painted that on the top of a hill, tied down with ropes because it was quite windy at the top.

That's very unusual for you, isn't it?

Very unusual, and this other *Red Hill, Anticoli II (Pl.37)* – it's a bit of the same landscape – that was done partly outside and finished in the studio. It's a more abstracted one; it's more stylised anyway – but because of this kind of broken technique that I was using which actually seemed to express the rockiness of the landscape, I think I got something out of landscape which I had never got before. It allowed me to use colour a little bit more freely to begin with. This is really fairly exaggerated – the actual place wasn't a colourful landscape.

You are quoted as saying to a Dundee Courier *reporter that you are not really a landscape painter because you tend to work in your studio from sketches.*

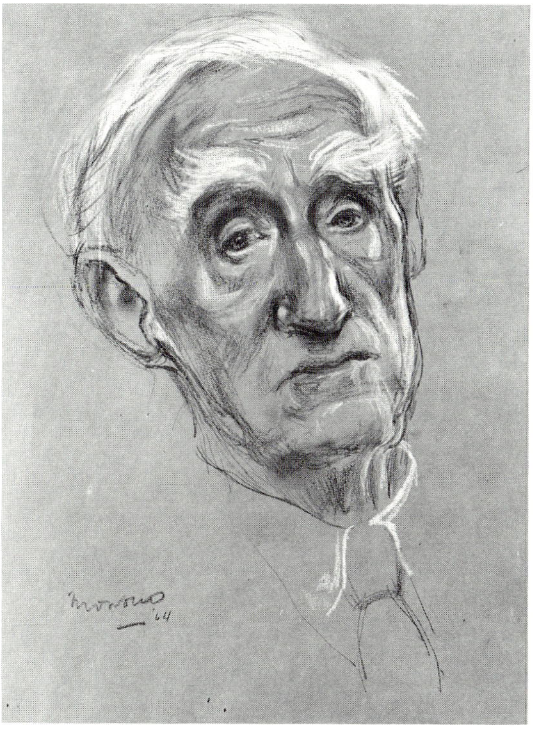

Plate 48 *The Rt Hon Lord Boyd Orr of Brechin,* 1964 (Cat.71)

Well, that also is true. That group of paintings is the only time I have ever done any serious landscape painting on any sort of scale. But I've painted landscape as a sketcher all my life. I started as a student painter – I used to go out every weekend painting a couple of panels per day – I'd cycle for hours looking for something ready-made as a painting, until I discovered that wasn't the way to do it; you painted what was there and looked at the landscape as something that you could react to.

Still-life painting is very dominant in your work today. When did it really take off?

Well, I have painted still-life off and on throughout my career but I really started concentrating on it about fifteen years ago. It seemed to me to serve a very useful purpose at the time, which

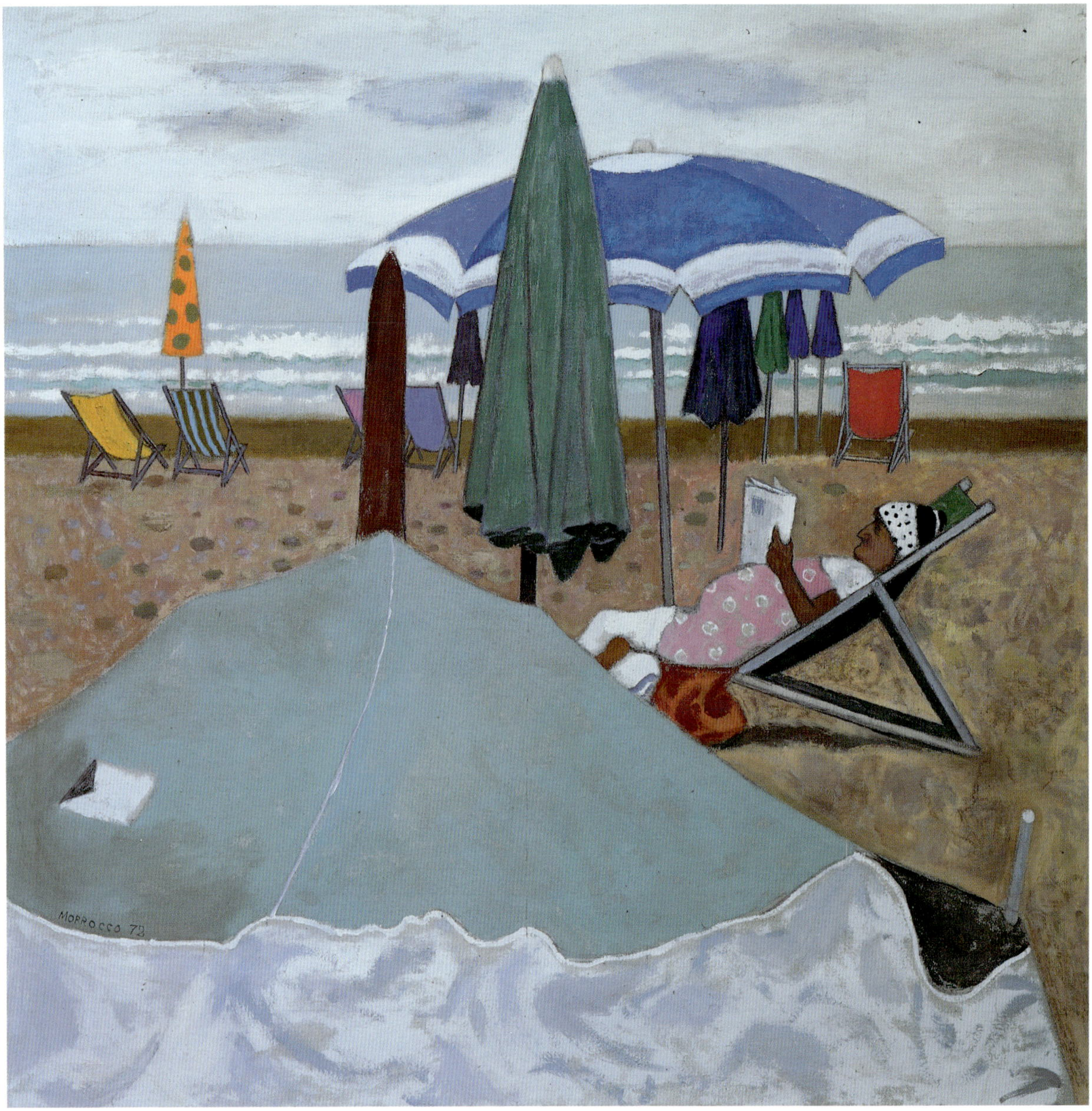

Plate 49 *Dull Day at the Lido*, 1972 (Cat.93)

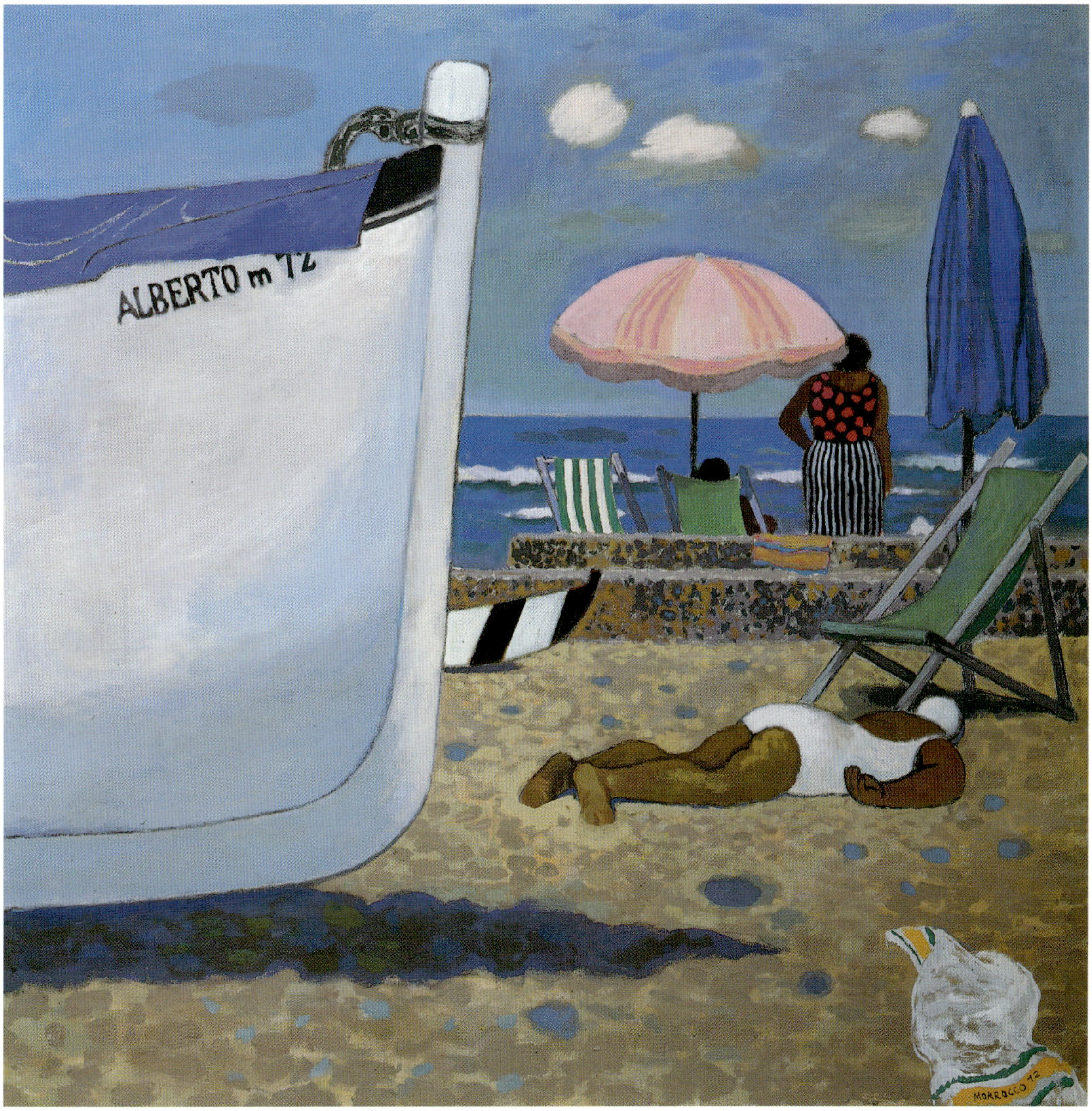

Plate 50 *Fine Day at the Lido*, 1972 (Cat.94)

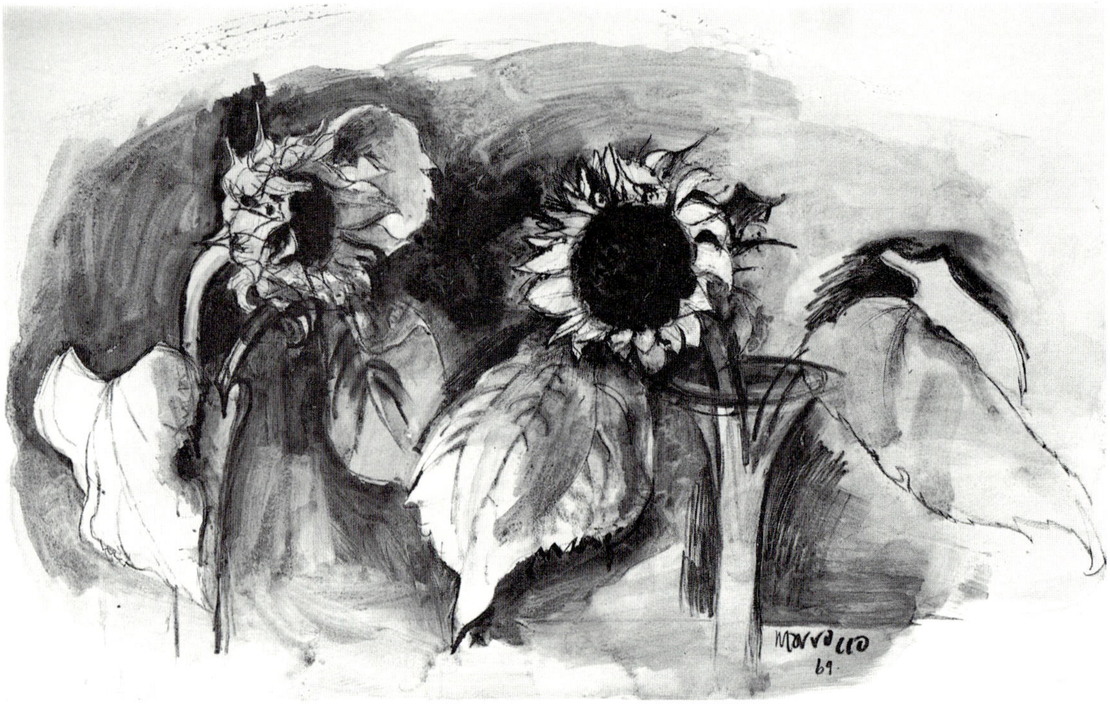

Plate 51 *Sunflowers*, 1969 (Cat.80)

was to establish a pattern of working in which one could have something ongoing at the same time as one was doing other things. If I was doing, say, something including figures or even a portrait, I would have a still-life set up during that period so that there were no gaps between. I wasn't waiting to think up some other idea. The other thing, of course, was that I became much more conscious of the formal values that a still-life can actually give freedom for – so that I began to look at still-life from this point of view, not simply depicting a few apples or oranges or a couple of jugs and so forth, as a kind of theme – but simply the relationship of the shape of a jug to the shape of a compote or the shape of a pear or the colour of a few objects on a white tablecloth against something in the background. You can actually use the shapes within a still-life just as you would in an abstract because they don't necessarily have to tell any story – apart from their own existence. From that point of view I think it's a very valuable part of any contemporary artist's work, if he or she is a figurative painter.

One picture painted in 1991 is actually called Homage à Braque (Pl.82). *Is he an influence?*

Not really. I've never admired him like I admire Picasso or Matisse. He is a much quieter character – much more reserved – a beautiful colourist in a reserved kind of field. But in one or two of the still-lifes I was doing I began to see things happening which related to Braque's colour. If I am using strong colour over a long period, I eventually become almost sated with powerful colour and feel a need to refresh myself by using colour in a sort of minor key as a kind of relief – it's almost a physical thing. This picture suggests something like the kind of colour that Braque was using and I introduced as a result a bird which he often used as a kind of hint that this was taking place.

With regard to figurative painting there are certain themes in your work that recur again and again with variations – such as peasants on a beach; women leaning out of windows; the sleeping melon-seller. What are the origins of these favourite subjects?

Well, it goes back quite a bit actually – it's when I first started going regularly to Italy in the early 1950s and making lots and lots of sketchbook drawings. I used to walk around the streets and anything that caught my eye which I reacted to I just drew. I used to draw mainly in line and make written colour notes to remind me of what I saw. I used to see things like the melon-sellers which is a favourite subject I have used quite often. One used to see in Rome in particular in front of the station – the Termini – two or three of these melon-sellers with great blocks of ice and the melons on top. I am a great lover of melon in the first place – I like the fruit to eat – I broke the record: I ate fourteen slices one night, one very hot night in Rome. Anyway, I made lots of drawings of that as well.

These subjects that I used to see in Italy, which you don't see here – the human figure related to something that's happening either in their work or whatever. I mean, they live out of doors, so that one is able to use the human figure on beaches to begin with – almost the nude figure in all kinds of attitudes in relation to the eternal sea, the strip of blue or green that's in front against the sky; the abstraction of this strip of sand, this strip of sea and strip of sky in varying proportions splitting the canvas into three sections [referring to *Peasants on a Beach (Pl.86)*] and then intervening, linking it, knitting a pattern through it with figures intrigues me a lot – I mean, that abstract background to the thing first of all. But then the subject also interests me. And because I'm of Italian origin and I react to the kind of lifestyle naturally, these subjects I've chosen to paint are the subjects which are near to my heart.

How many sleeping melon-sellers did you see?

Well, actually, I didn't see any. I mean, when you view reality and make sketches one is prepared to actually change it to the *possible* rather than the *actual*. What you have seen is probably a starting point, rather than a finishing point. I saw one of the melon-sellers half-dozing, sitting relaxed in front of his slices of water-melon. That gave me the idea, and I have simply juggled around the material from drawings mainly until I found some satisfactory picture-making theme to get out of it. The mural I did at Liff Hospital shows one of the initial uses of that particular theme.

How important is Italy to you as a painter?

Very important. If I were to be absolutely honest and dig down into my own reasons for painting Italian things, one of the reasons is certainly that I don't want to lose the link with my background. I feel more in touch when I paint these things.

When did you really feel that you had found yourself as an artist? The Alberto Morrocco we know today – when did he come into being?

I really don't know if I could answer that question. Even today I am not so very sure if I have found myself. I mean, I have had a constant struggle throughout my career to try and find a central kind of viewpoint which is mine only. Being versatile is one of the most difficult things to contend with. I used to see it with the students: occasionally you got a student who was able in lots of directions and the choice this student had to make was much more difficult than that of some of the other students who could only do one thing and therefore didn't have the difficulty of being diverted from the main source of their inspiration. I could think of lots of painters like this, quite successful painters who have got one idea. I can take just one from the past: Modigliani – he was a limited painter in one sense. He painted the nude – he never painted landscapes, interiors or groups of figures. He painted a single figure either as a portrait or a reclining figure – that was his language. What he

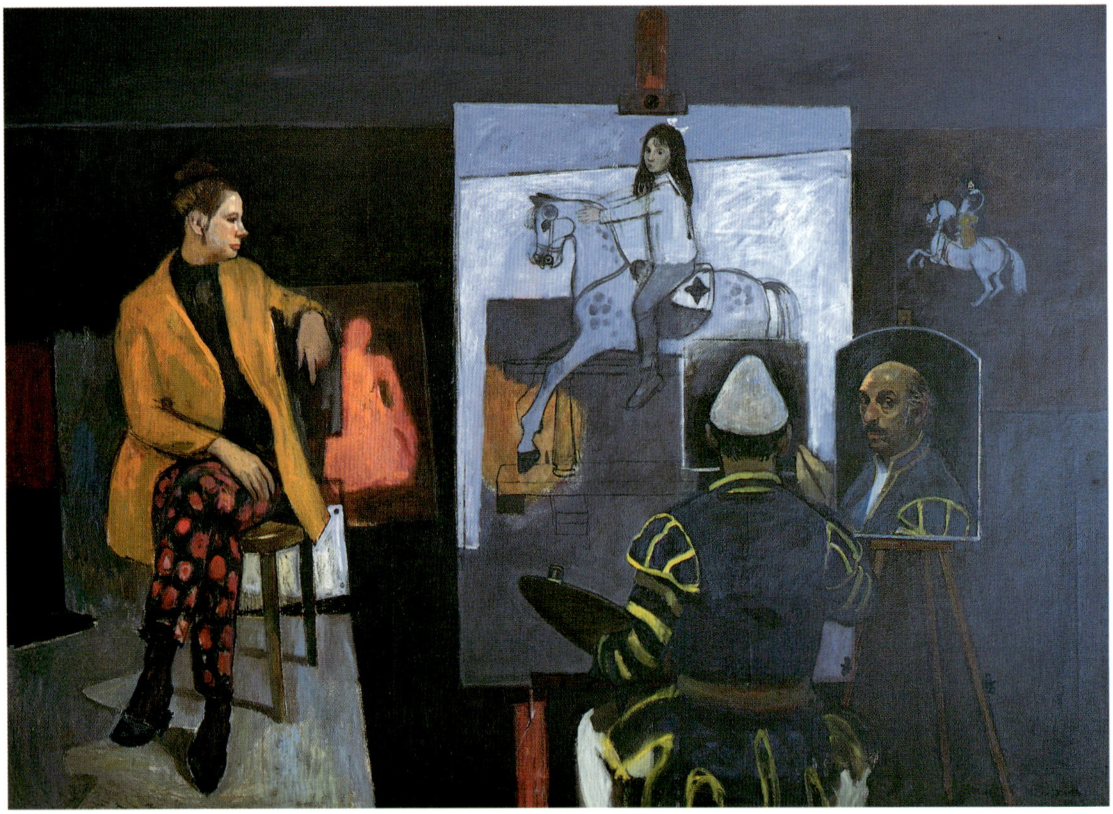

Plate 52 *Self-portrait with Wife and Child and Conde, Duque de Olivares*, c.1968 (Cat.79)

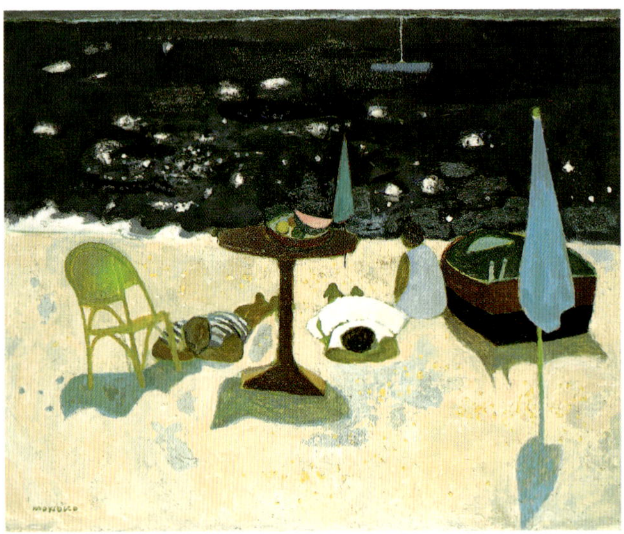

Plate 53 *The Beach at Stromboli*, c.1970 (Cat.87)

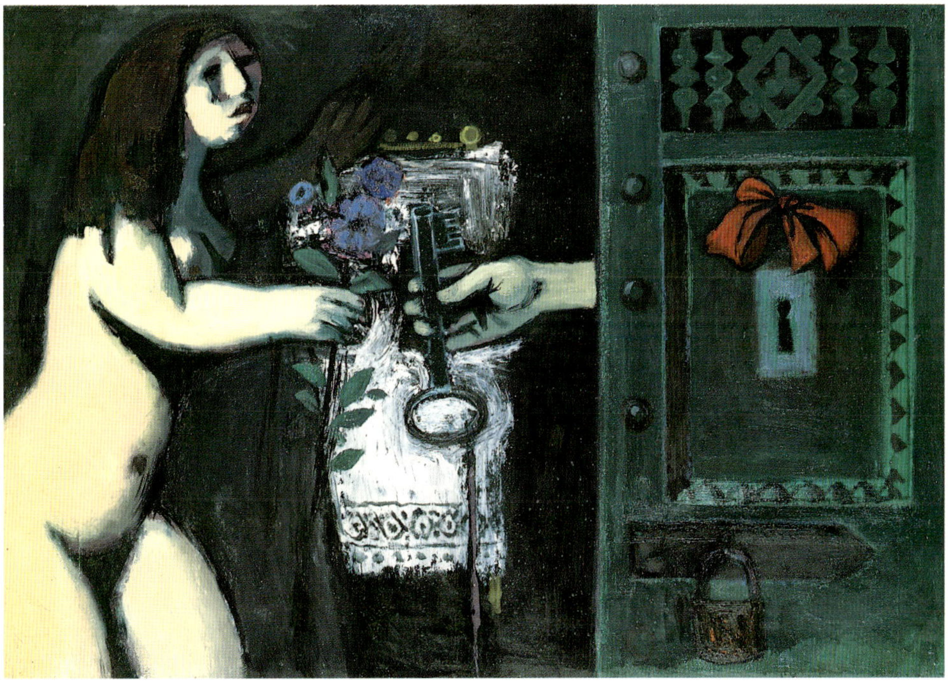

Plate 54 *The Key (Mariage de Convenance)*, 1969 (Cat.82)

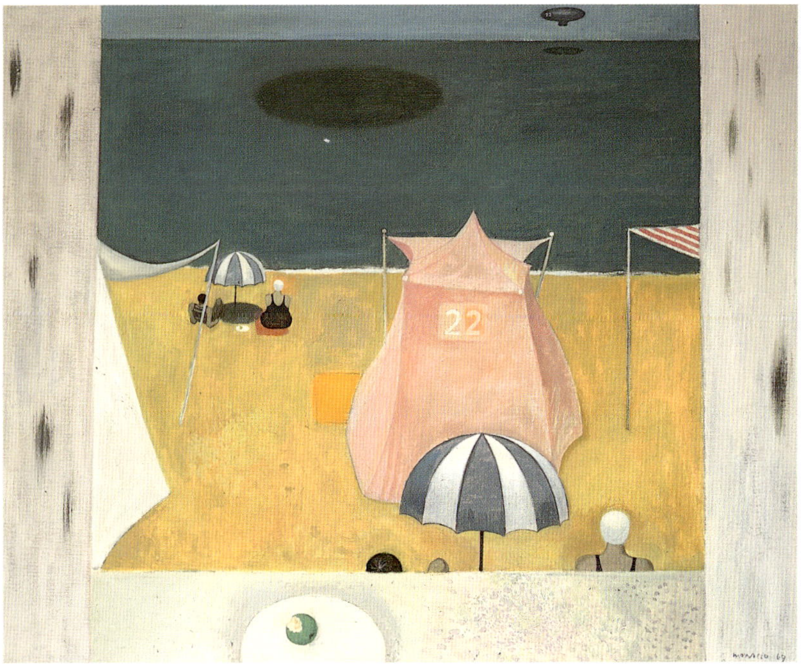

Plate 55 *Dirigible over Deauville*, 1969 (Cat.84)

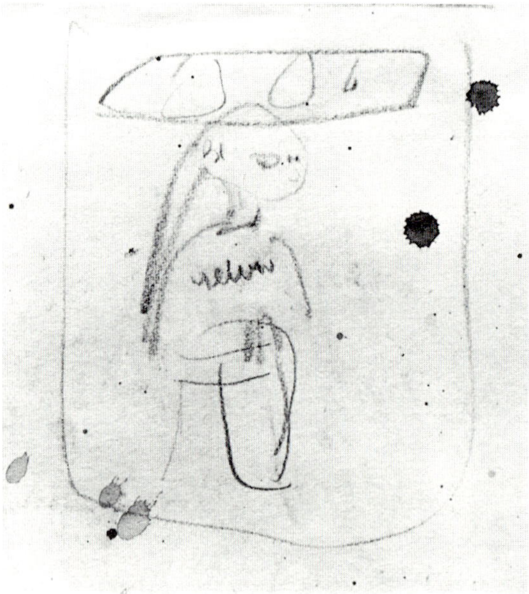

Plate 56 Five-second sketch for *Girl with Laundry*, 1950s

did with the language was incredible – he's a great painter. That's a different kind of painter from me. As I said before, I see a lot of diverse kinds of subject matter – I react to things which are almost opposed to each other in style. That is difficult to contend with, but as I have got older – I can't really put a date to it – I gradually began to centralise the thing. My Italian background was the main kind of influence because it all centred round actually making contact back to where I came from.

We are looking at this photograph of the big mural at Liff (Pl.90). *To me this looks very much like mature Morrocco.*

That's right. I put everything into this mural; it's an amalgam of all the kind of things I had been doing, if you like. I took bits from pictures; I took things from drawings I had done; I took things from memory. One thing led to another in this mural – I had a grand sketch full of things to begin with. But I diverted from it as I went on because on the wall itself I began to see other possibilities. This macho Italian bather sitting on the right here is typical: it exemplifies the kind of Italian young man, the Italian character in a sense. People sleeping in boats, a woman drying a child's feet, boats in the background – people active on this sandy-coloured beach.

The drawing here is already quite stylised, isn't it?

Yes it is. Again, working from drawing I discovered early that, if one were actually going to make something which had a personal direction to it, you couldn't stick to a drawing which had been done directly from nature. If you did that it would simply become your recording rather than putting a point of view on the thing. So I gradually evolved a type – a type of woman, a type of boy, a type of man, all related to each other in this particular style. I mean, hands are big and muscles are overdone, if you like; the boys are thin or skinny, or the women are plump with babies. I didn't think that up – it happened just by observation really, and by exaggeration and selection.

Would you agree that your work is hedonistic – full of pleasure?

Yes, I would agree with that. I suppose I agree partly with Matisse when he said that his ambition in his work was to try and make a painting which was like a good armchair to relax in. I think there is something in that – he wasn't involved in angst; he didn't want to introduce what he called 'unpleasant' subject matter. He liked the beautiful things in nature and I think I am inclined that way as well.

Yet there's another slightly sinister aspect to your work in the rather surreal paintings of the 1960s, like The Key (Pl.54). *Occasionally big knives appear. In this early picture of c.1958* [Interior with a Hungry Cat (Pl.26)], *an enormous knife is stuck into a fish.*

That's true. Again, I am not a totally unified character. I mean, I have certain dispositions towards the pleasant things but every so often I want to do something a little less conformist in that respect. In still-life I use knives because of their beautiful shape – especially the knives one sees abroad, these cutting knives which have a rather fierce look about them, a triangular blade with a rather more decorative handle. Often when I am doing things with fruit, I like to lay a knife near the fruit: a soft pear against a sharp knife has got a kind of a *frisson* about it, I think, and I often stick the knife into a water-melon because the two things have got a rather nice abstract thing – a vertical or almost vertical shape – sticking into a kind of semi-circular shape that in itself satisfies.

There is something just a touch cruel, ugly, in The Blind Fortune-teller (Pl.38).

Well, again that's a reversal from the things I'd probably been doing previous to that. The fortune-teller with the monkey is something I saw in Sicily in the 1950s. It is nothing like a portrait of the man – it is really a memory of the idea and me emphasising the blindness. It relates back to another picture called *I Poveri*, which is dealing with something which wasn't a pleasantry, and I was trying to get something of that into the painting – something a bit more serious as a bit of expression.

And even Boy with Bowl of Eggs (Pl.43) *obviously depicts poverty.*

Yes, a skinny boy. I used to see a lot of that in Sicily at that time and the fact of making a kind of contrast of this boy with the large white bowl with eggs in it seemed to me to have some kind of relationship which was interesting.

Now in the 1960s you did a lot of experimental work – constructions, abstracts, sculptures – junk sculpture.

The junk sculpture thing: again I suppose the whole idea of construction came from Picasso – he was one of the first, anyway. The idea of using existing objects which suggest another object – a real object, a head or a figure or whatever – is what makes the thing interesting. I used to sit on

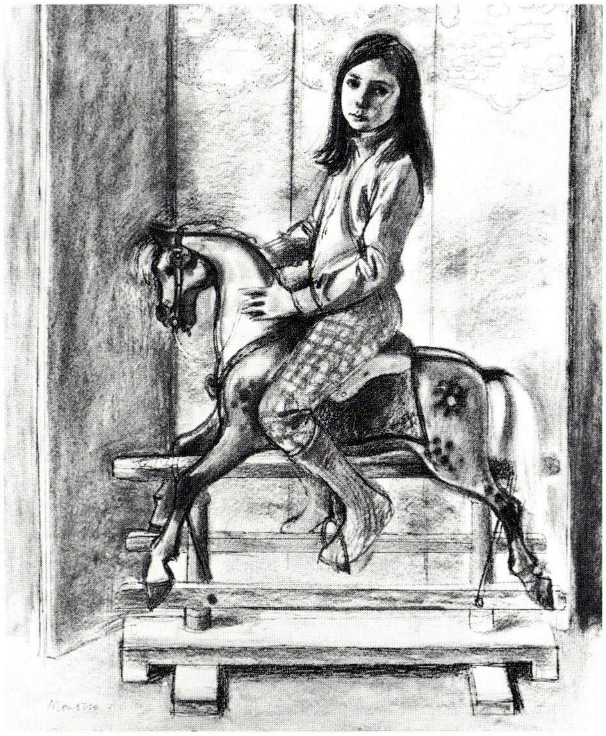

Plate 57 *Lisa on Hobbyhorse*, 1971 (Cat.91)

the beach in various places I've been with a bag of tools – a chisel, a hammer, nails, glue, a saw and some Stanley knives – to whittle a bit and go along the beach and pick up bits of boats and *bric-à-brac* one could find on beaches abroad.

You had a show at the Compass Gallery in 1969.

I had a show of some of these things I did then and I got quite ambitious. A group of pop musicians was one of the things which I tackled at that time. In fact, I have always been interested in sculpture – I nearly specialised in it as a student, I was almost on the verge of doing sculpture instead of painting but I think the idea of giving up colour swung me the other way.

Now, you are still painting very enthusiastically – almost compulsively – that's right? You have one-man shows booked ahead until 1995. What still motivates you today?

The idea of painting. The best and healthiest way

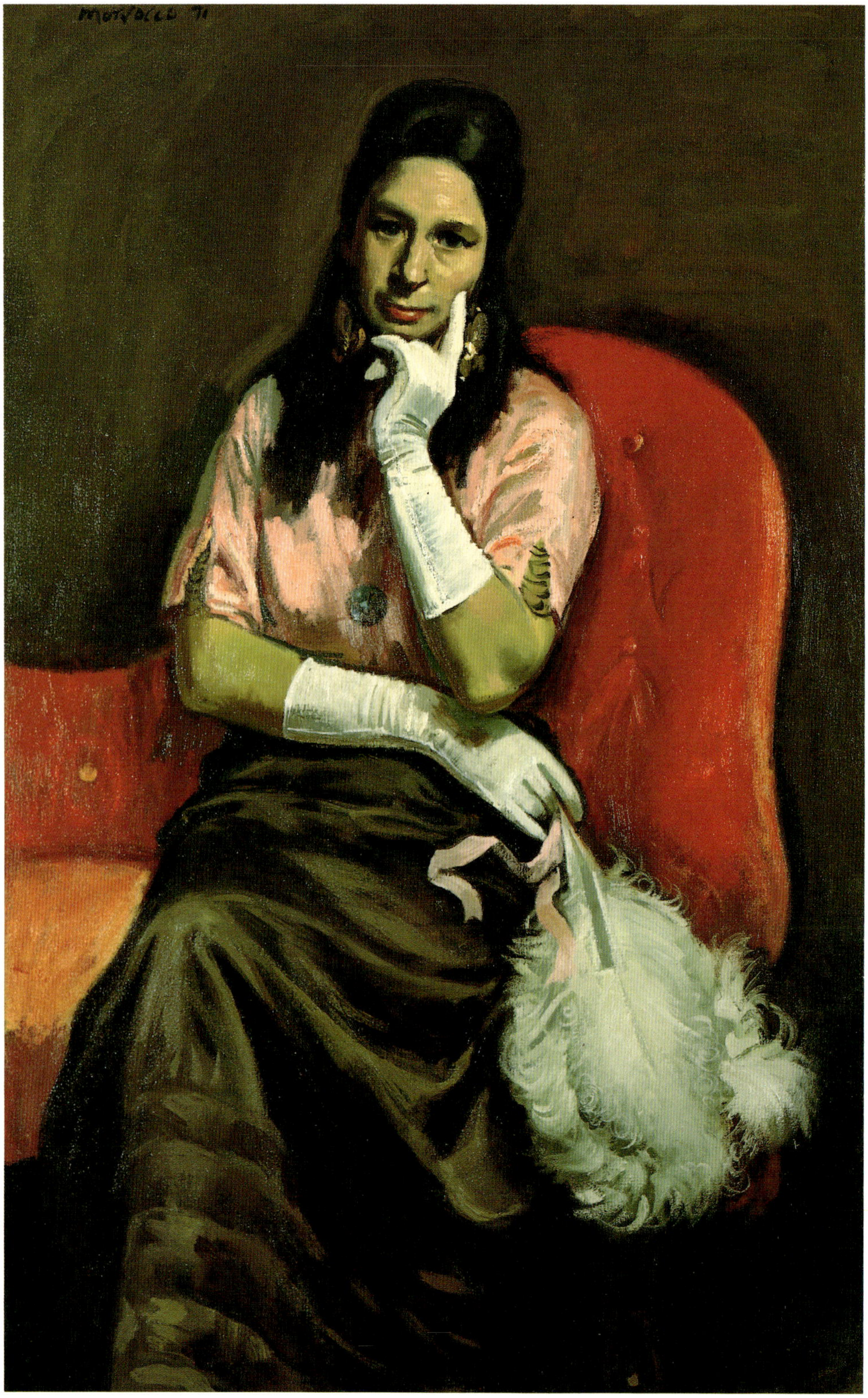

Plate 58 *Portrait of Vera*, 1971 (Cat.88)

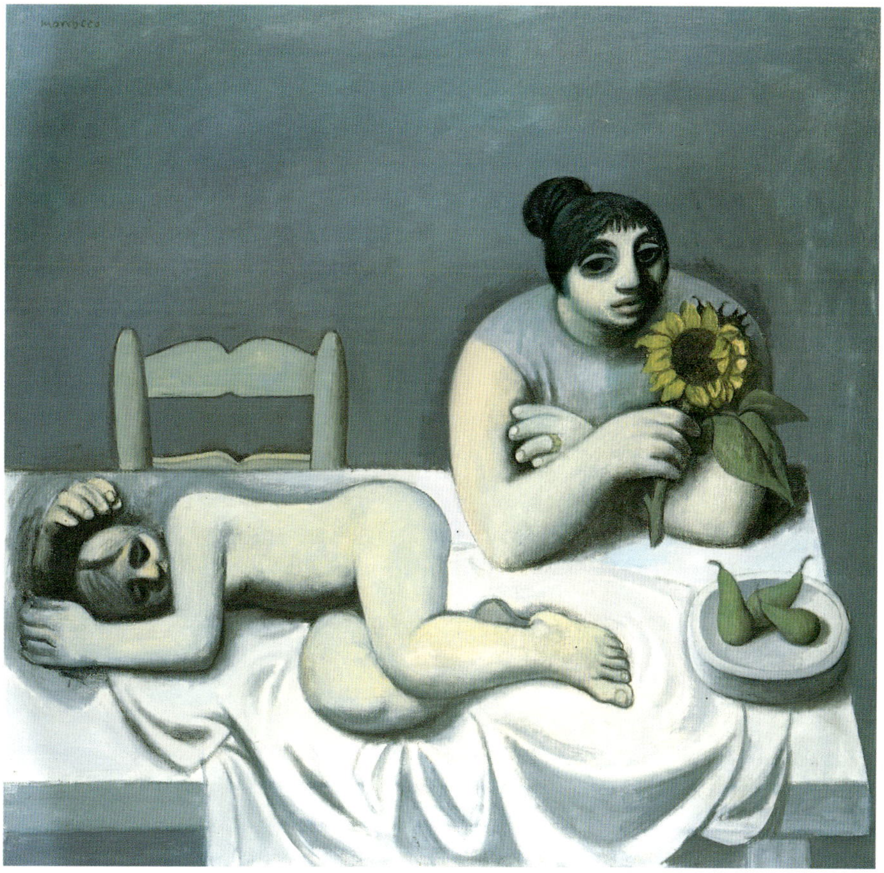

Plate 59 *Siesta*, c.1971 (Cat.90)

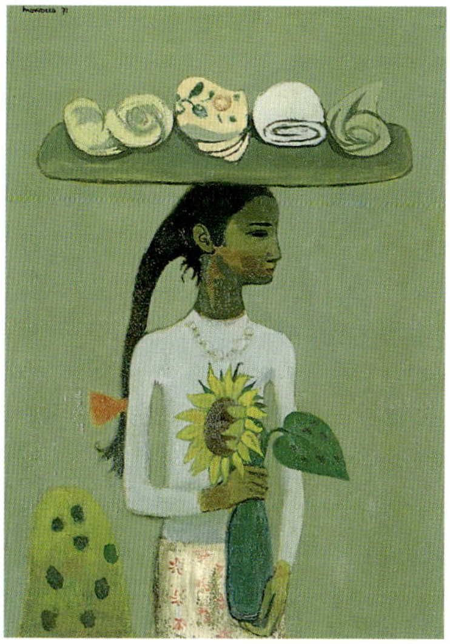

Plate 60 *Girl with Laundry*, 1971 (Cat.89)

of approaching painting is simply to paint every day, whatever happens with the things, whatever success one has. That isn't always possible but I mean that's what one attempts to do – and when one is having a one-man exhibition, as I mentioned earlier, one is committed to a certain date and then one's professionalism takes over. You have periods in which things don't quite come off – that can become quite stressful, actually. But the idea of doing better than you have done before – that's what makes one tick in a sense. There's something extra that you can add even to a theme which you have done before – and so it is always renewing and reflecting itself. One always has the feeling that one can do better than one did before.

During my career I've used the human figure in portraits, in nudes and in subject pictures and so forth. Now at my age, at this point in my career, I feel a need to direct most of my energies into concentrating on the single human figure almost specifically.

Do you feel driven?

Yes, in a sense I do feel driven. Time is short to begin with – I've always felt that. Now that I'm older I feel it very strongly. But even when I was younger I thought, 'Well, my God, I'll have to get on with this – I'm now in my thirties and I haven't done too much. I'd better get on with this and see if I can produce something.' I've felt driven all my life in that respect.

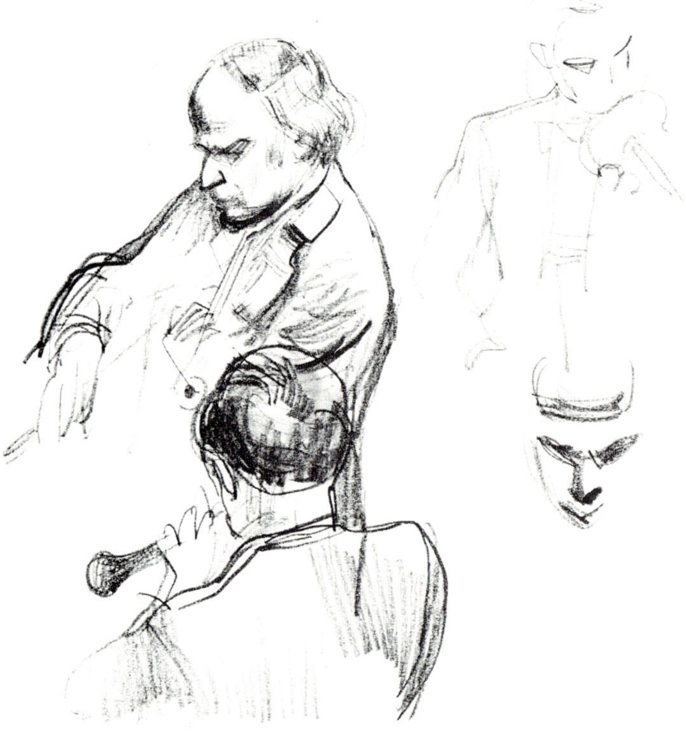

Plate 61 Original sketch for *Yehudi Menuhin*

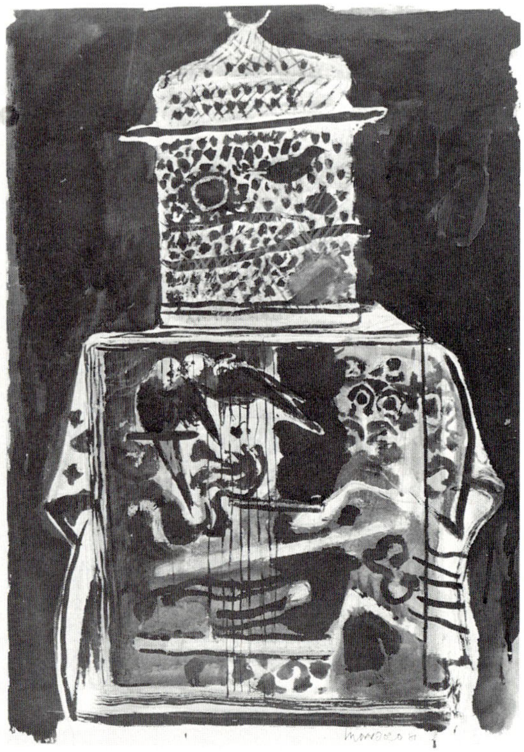

Plate 62 *Caged Birds at Night*, 1981 (Cat.126)

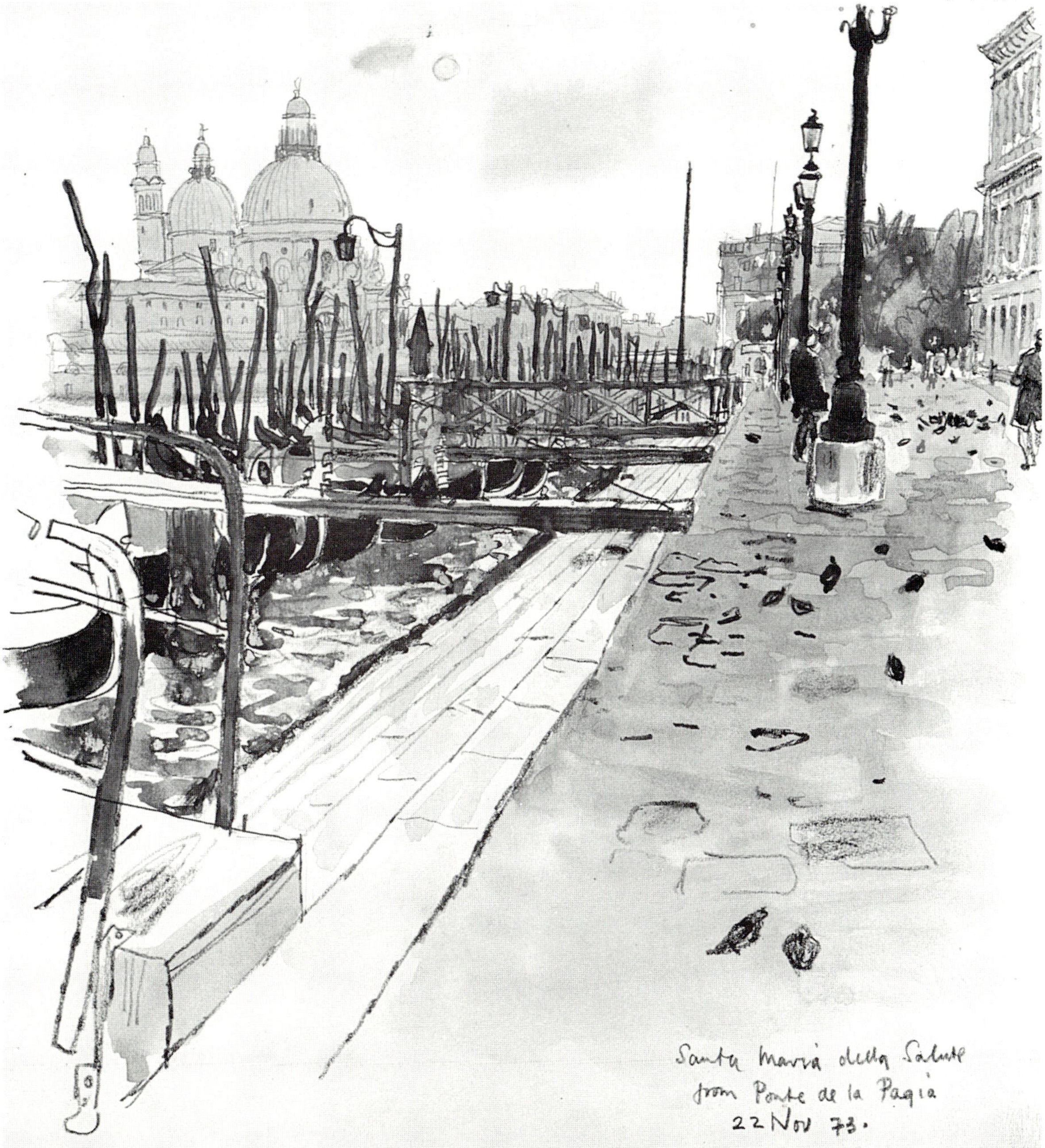

Plate 63 *Fondamenta Pescheria, Burano*, 1973 (Cat.99)

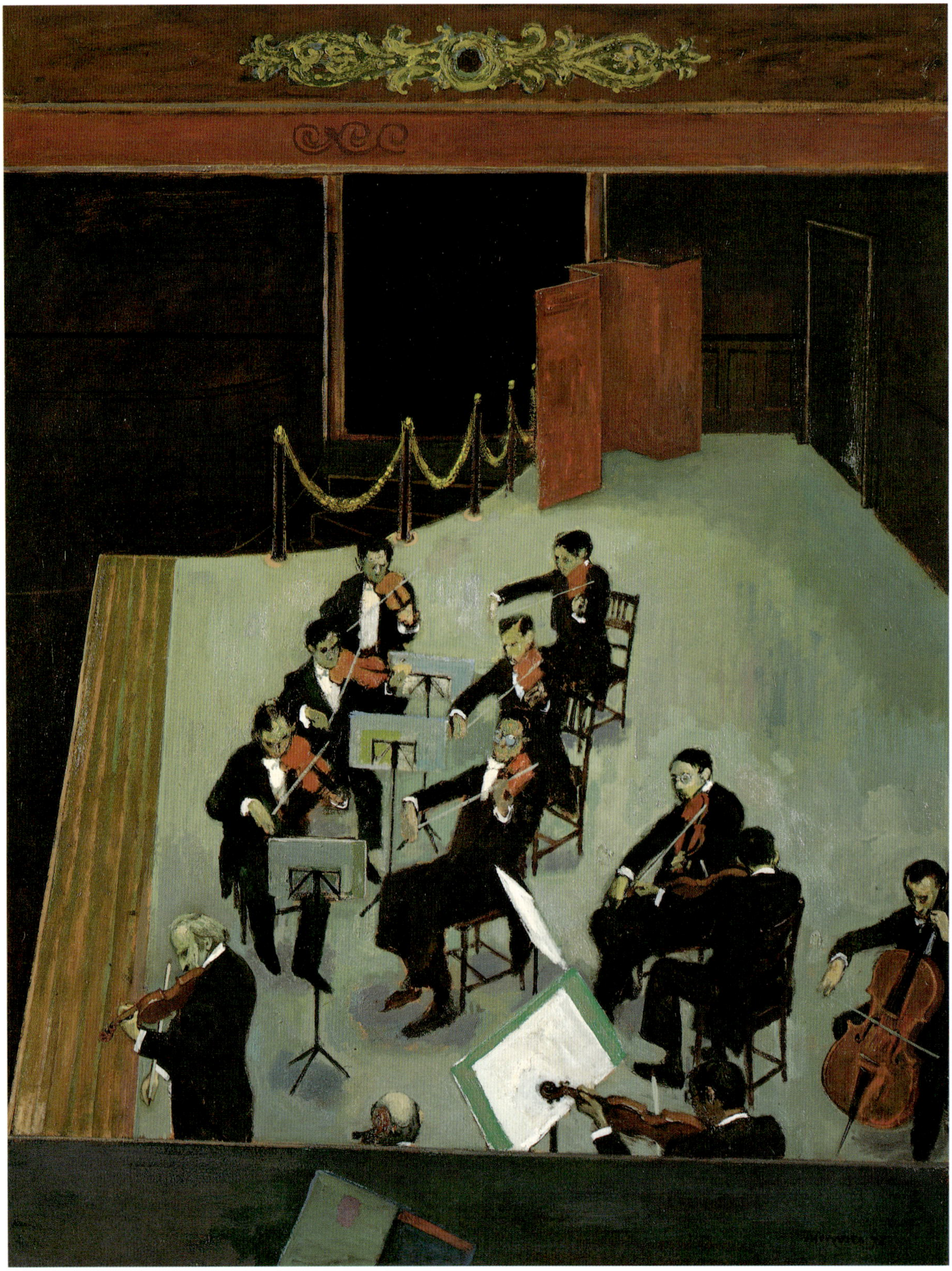

Plate 64 *Yehudi Menuhin at the Caird Hall*, 1972 (Cat.92)

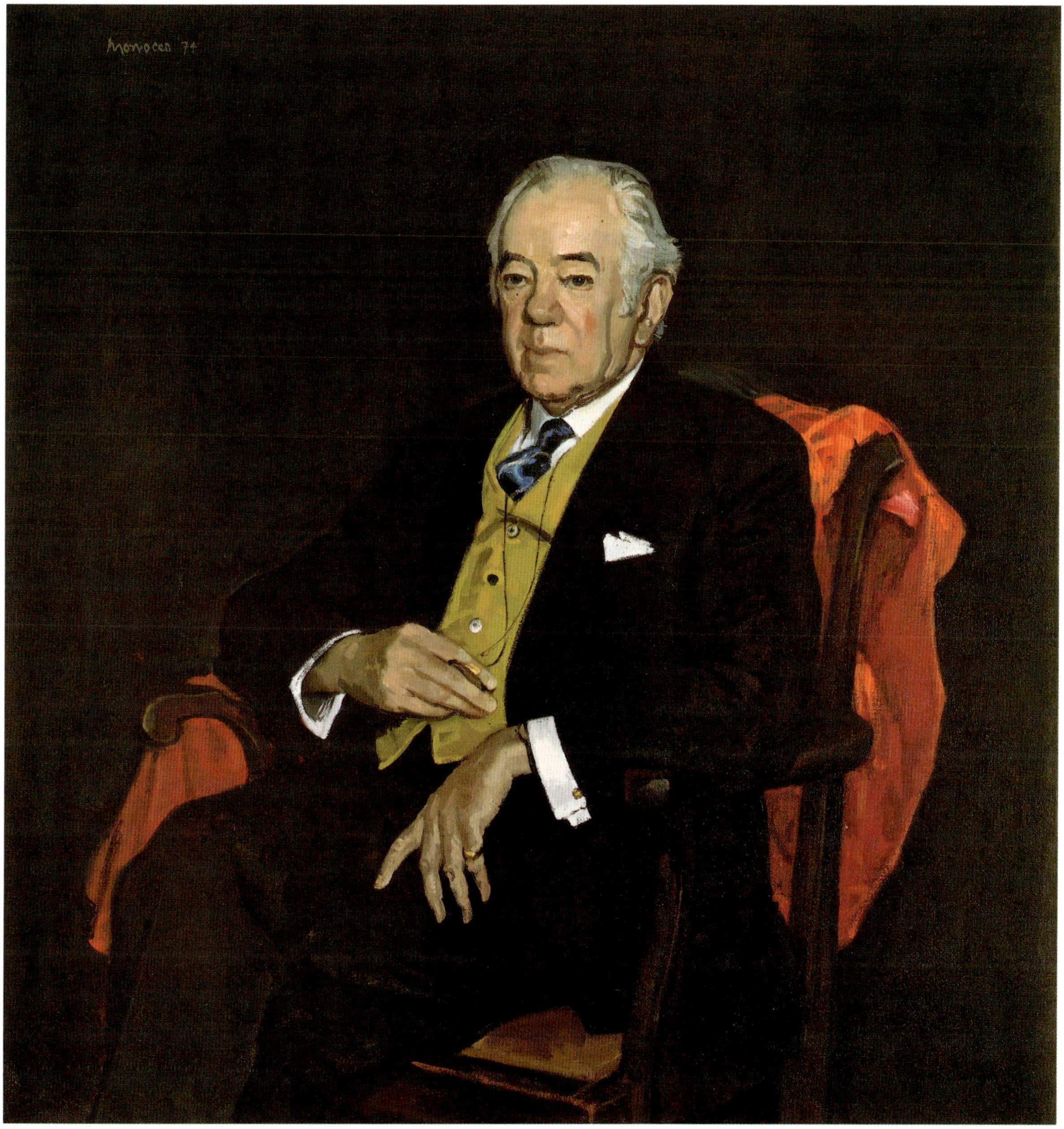

Plate 65 *The Honourable Lord Cameron*, 1974 (Cat.105)

BIOGRAPHY

1917	Born in Aberdeen, of Italian parents
1932-38	Studied at Gray's School of Art, Aberdeen
	Awarded Brough Travelling Scholarship and Carnegie Travelling Scholarship
1938-39	Assisted Robert Sivell on the murals for the University of Aberdeen Students' Union
1939	Studied and travelled in France and Switzerland
	Exhibited at the Royal Scottish Academy for the first time
1940-46	Army service
1941	Marriage to Vera Mercer
1942	Birth of first child, Leon
1943	Guthrie Award, Royal Scottish Academy
1946-49	Taught part-time, Gray's School of Art, Aberdeen
1947	Founder member of Aberdeen's '47 Group'
	Birth of second son, Laurie
1947-49	Illustrated *Lockhart's Anatomy* with R. W. Matthews, Gordon S. Cameron, Donald J. Stephen and William Cruikshank (published by Faber & Faber, 1959)
1950	First trip to Italy after the war, to finish travelling scholarship
1950-82	Head of Painting, Duncan of Jordanstone College of Art, Dundee
1951	Elected Associate of Royal Scottish Academy
1952	First trip to Spain
1957	Awarded Medaglia d'oro, San Vito, Italy
1960	Birth of daughter, Anna Lisa
1962	Elected Member of Royal Scottish Academy
1962-64	Painted mural for St Columba's Church, Glenrothes
1964-66	Painted two murals for Liff Hospital, Dundee
1965	Elected Member of Royal Scottish Society of Painters in Watercolours
1973	Visit to Venice in the winter, making studies for 'proposed portrait of the city'
1974	Tour of American art schools and collections
1975	Elected Member of Royal Society of Portrait Painters
1977	Elected Member of Royal Glasgow Institute
1980	Honorary Doctorate, University of Dundee
1984	Trip to Tunisia
1986	Trip to China
1987	Honorary Doctorate, University of Stirling
1993	Received the OBE

SOLO EXHIBITIONS

1949	British Council Gallery, Aberdeen
1955	Roseangle Gallery, Dundee
1957	The Scottish Gallery, Edinburgh
1962	Saltire Society Gallery, Edinburgh
1966	University of Dundee
1969	Compass Gallery, Glasgow
1969	University of Strathclyde, Glasgow

1971	Loomshop Gallery, Lower Largo
1973	Roseangle Gallery, Dundee
1973	The Scottish Gallery, Edinburgh
1974	Lamp of Lothian Gallery, Haddington
1976	Loomshop Gallery, Lower Largo
1978	Guest Artist, Dundee Art Society Biennial, Dundee City Art Gallery
1978	Stirling Gallery
1980	Thackeray Gallery, London
1981	Retrospective, Artspace Gallery, Aberdeen
1981	The English Speaking Union Gallery, Edinburgh
1982	The Macaulay Gallery, Stenton
1983	Thackeray Gallery, London
1984	Loomshop Gallery, Lower Largo
1985	Thackeray Gallery, London
1987	Festival Exhibition, The Scottish Gallery, Edinburgh
1988	Thackeray Gallery, London
1989	The Scottish Gallery, Edinburgh
1990	Thackeray Gallery, London
1990	The Scottish Gallery, Edinburgh
1992	Thackeray Gallery, London
1993	Major Retrospective Exhibition, Dundee Art Galleries and Museums, touring to Aberdeen Art Gallery, Edinburgh City Art Centre and the Lillie Art Gallery, Milngavie

SELECTED GROUP EXHIBITIONS

1939	Royal Scottish Academy, Edinburgh
1941-93	Royal Scottish Academy, Edinburgh
1947-50	'47 Group', Aberdeen Art Gallery
1962	'Artists of Anticoli', Galleria La Feluca, Rome
1964	'Four Scottish Artists', Arts Council Festival Exhibition, Edinburgh
1965	'Fourteen Scottish Painters', Commonwealth Institute, London
1967	'Scottish Painting', Munich
1970	'Five Dundee Painters', Edinburgh City Art Centre
1977	Pieter Weaning Gallery, Johannesburg
1978	'Painters in Parallel', Scottish Arts Council Exhibition, Edinburgh Festival
1981-82	'Contemporary Art from Scotland', Scottish Gallery (Touring)
1988	'The Scottish Show', an Oriel 31 touring exhibition
1989	'Scottish Painters', Fosse Gallery
1990	'RSA Guthrie Award Winners', The Fine Art Society, Glasgow

EXHIBITED IN MANY GROUP EXHIBITIONS AT

Loomshop Gallery, Lower Largo
The Open Eye Gallery, Edinburgh
Royal Academy, London
Royal Glasgow Institute
Royal Scottish Society of Painters in Water-colour
Society of Scottish Artists
The Scottish Gallery, Edinburgh
Thackeray Gallery, London

WORKS IN PUBLIC AND CORPORATE COLLECTIONS

Aberdeen Art Gallery and Museums
Bank of Scotland
Bristol City Art Gallery
British Linen Bank
Clydesdale Bank PLC
Dumfriesshire Educational Trust Collection
Dundas and Wilson
Dundee Art Galleries and Museums

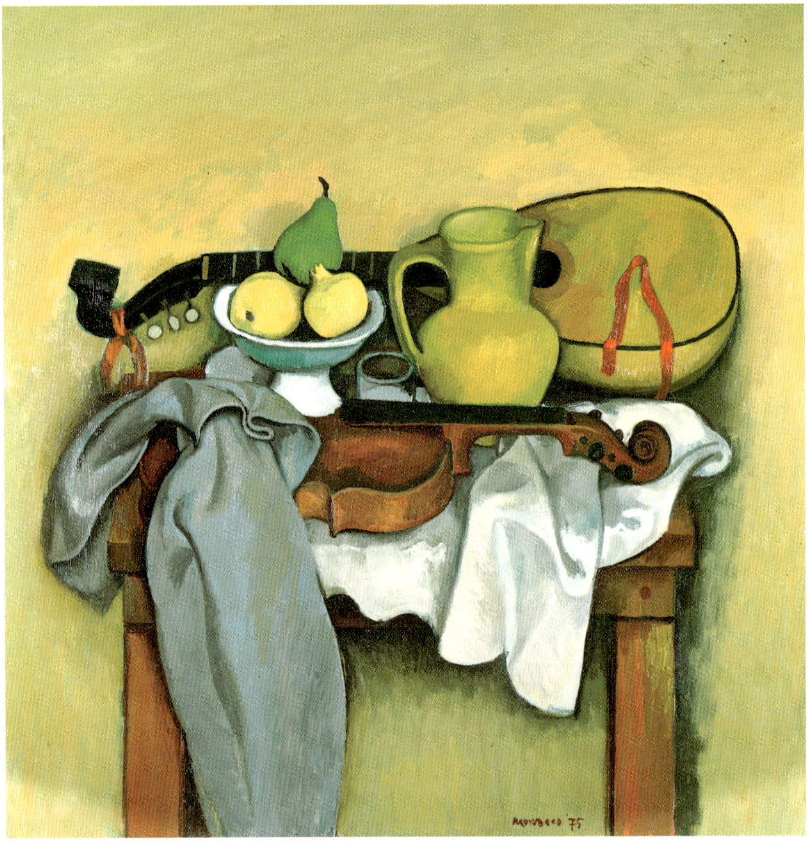

Plate 66 *Grande Natura Morta Napolitana*, 1975 (Cat.107)

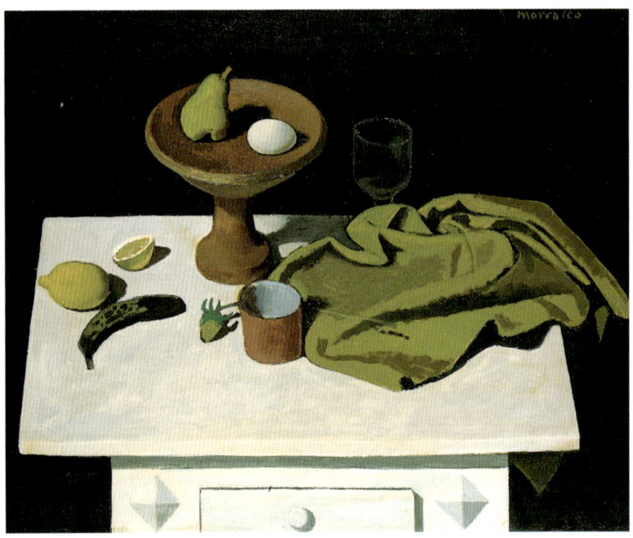

Plate 67 *Still-life with Fruit and Egg*, c.1974 (Cat.104)

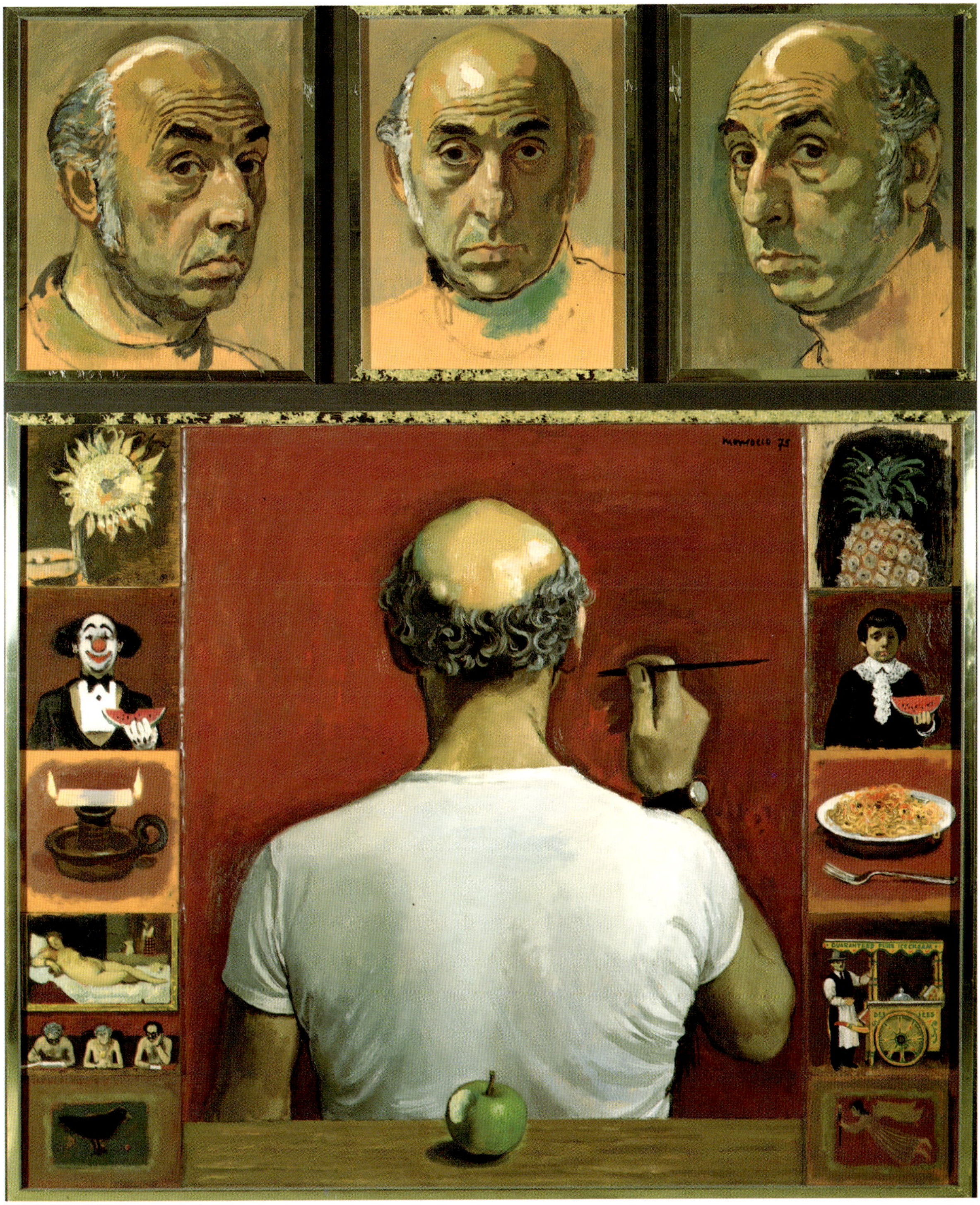

Plate 68 *Documentary Self-portrait*, 1975 (Cat.108)

The bottom left panel shows the RSA committee sitting in front of their copy of a Titian nude: in the centre, Sir Robin Philipson, PRSA, with James Cumming on his left. Other panels show: burning the candle at both ends; self-portrait as a clown; and self-portrait as a child dressed in Christmas finery.

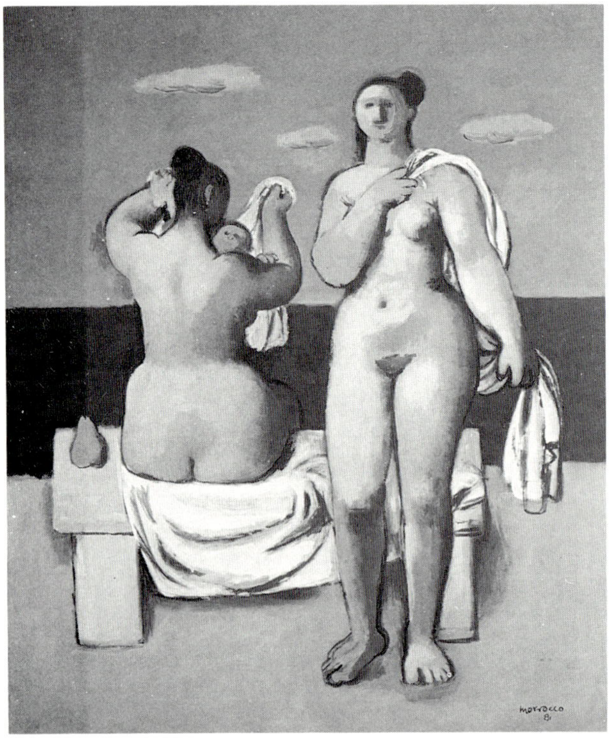

Plate 69 *Women by the Sea*, 1981 (Cat.127)

Dunedin Fund Managers, Edinburgh
Edinburgh City Art Centre
General Accident
Glasgow Art Galleries and Museums
Grampian Television PLC
Heriot-Watt University, Edinburgh
Icelandic Government Collection, Reykjavik
Kirkcaldy Art Gallery and Museum
Lillie Art Gallery, Milngavie
Low and Bonar PLC, Dundee
McLean Museum and Art Gallery, Greenock
National Galleries of Scotland
Newark on Trent Municipal Museum
Paisley Museum and Art Gallery
Perth Museum and Art Gallery
Robert Fleming Holdings Limited
Royal Bank of Scotland plc
Royal Scottish Academy
The *Scotsman* Newspaper
Scottish Arts Council Collection
Scottish Television
University of Aberdeen
University of Dundee
University of Edinburgh
University of Glasgow
University of Leicester
University of St Andrews
University of Stirling
West Riding County Council

SELECTED BIBLIOGRAPHY

MAGAZINE ARTICLES

Douglas Percy Bliss, 'Art in Scotland Now', *The Studio*, vol. 146, July-December 1953

Emilio Coia, 'Alberto Morrocco', *Scottish Field*, March 1967

Andrew Hannah, 'Scottish Colourists Today', *The Studio*, vol. 152, July-December 1956

David Phillips, 'A Life of Colour', *Scots Magazine*, vol. 79, no. 2, May 1963

EXHIBITION CATALOGUE TEXTS

Alice Bain, *New Paintings by Alberto Morrocco*, The Scottish Gallery, Edinburgh, 1987

John Cameron, *Alberto Morrocco*, Lamp of Lothian Collegiate Centre, Haddington House, Haddington, 1976

David McClure, *Four Scottish Artists: Blyth, Donaldson, Henderson, Morrocco*, The Arts Council Gallery, Edinburgh, 1964

David McClure, *Paintings from the Artist's Studio*, The Scottish Gallery, Edinburgh, 1990

Ian McKenzie Smith, *Alberto Morrocco Retrospective: 1954-1981*, Artspace Galleries, Aberdeen, 1981

Duncan Macmillan, *The Scottish Show*, Oriel 31 touring exhibition, 1988

Cordelia Oliver, *Painters in Parallel*, Edinburgh College of Art, 1978

REFERENCES IN BOOKS

Jack Firth, *Scottish Watercolour Painting* (Edinburgh, 1979)

Edward Gage, *The Eye in the Wind: Contemporary Scottish Painting Since 1945* (London, 1977)

Julian Halsby and Paul Harris, *The Dictionary of Scottish Painters: 1600-1960* (Edinburgh, 1990)

William Hardie, *Scottish Painting: 1837-Present* (London, 1990)

Duncan Macmillan, *Scottish Art 1460-1990*, (Edinburgh, 1990)

The Royal Scottish Academy Exhibitors 1826-1990, vol.3, L-Q (Edinburgh, 1991). This lists the 216 pictures that the artist exhibited at the RSA between 1939 and 1989

Frances Spalding, *The Dictionary of British Twentieth-Century Painters and Sculptors* (London, 1990)

Anne Wishart and Cordelia Oliver (eds.), *The Society of Scottish Artists: the First 100 Years* (Edinburgh, 1990)

TELEVISION

'Alberto Morrocco', *Talking Pictures*, Scottish Television, 1992

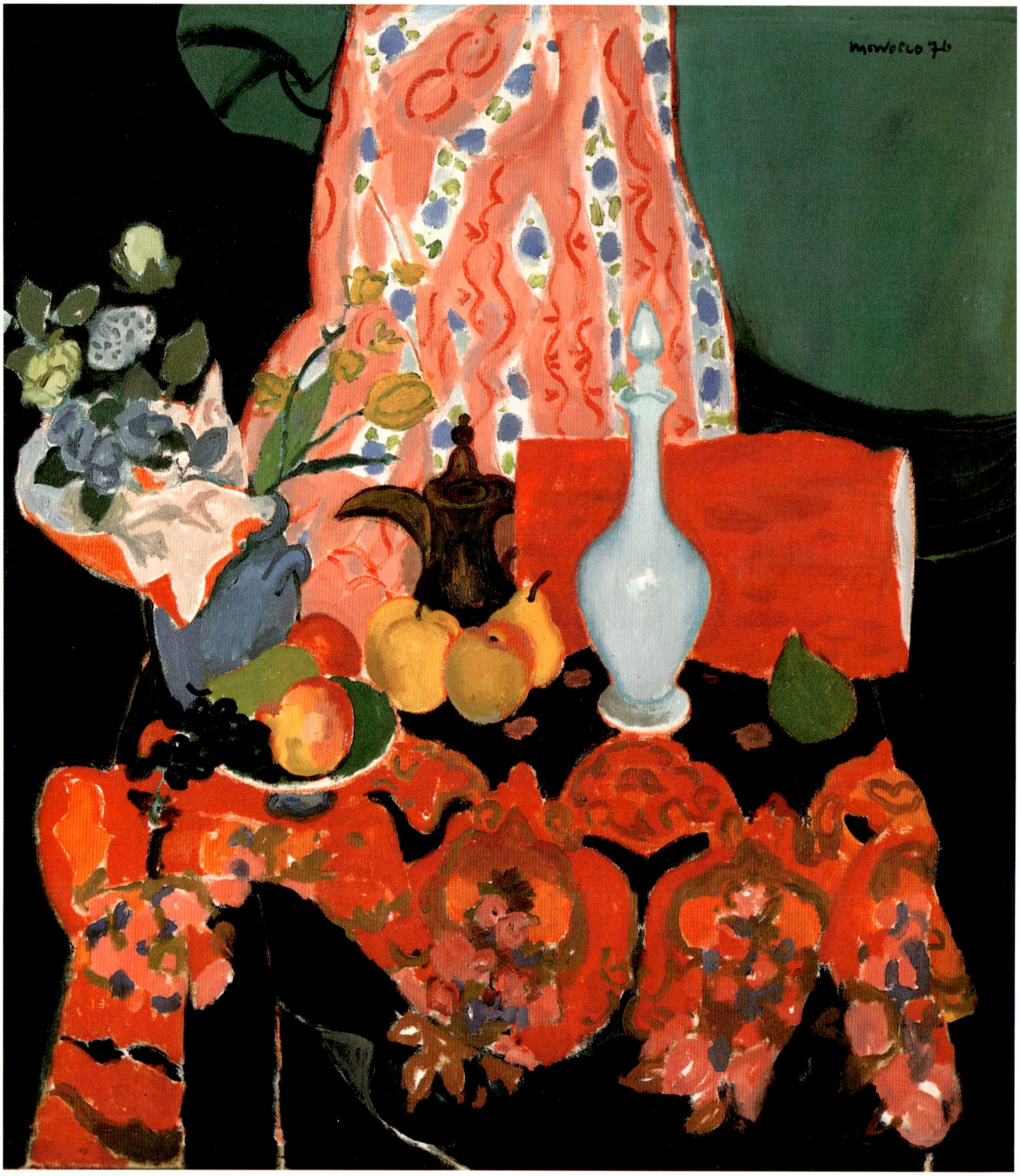

Plate 70 *Turcomania*, 1976 (Cat.110)

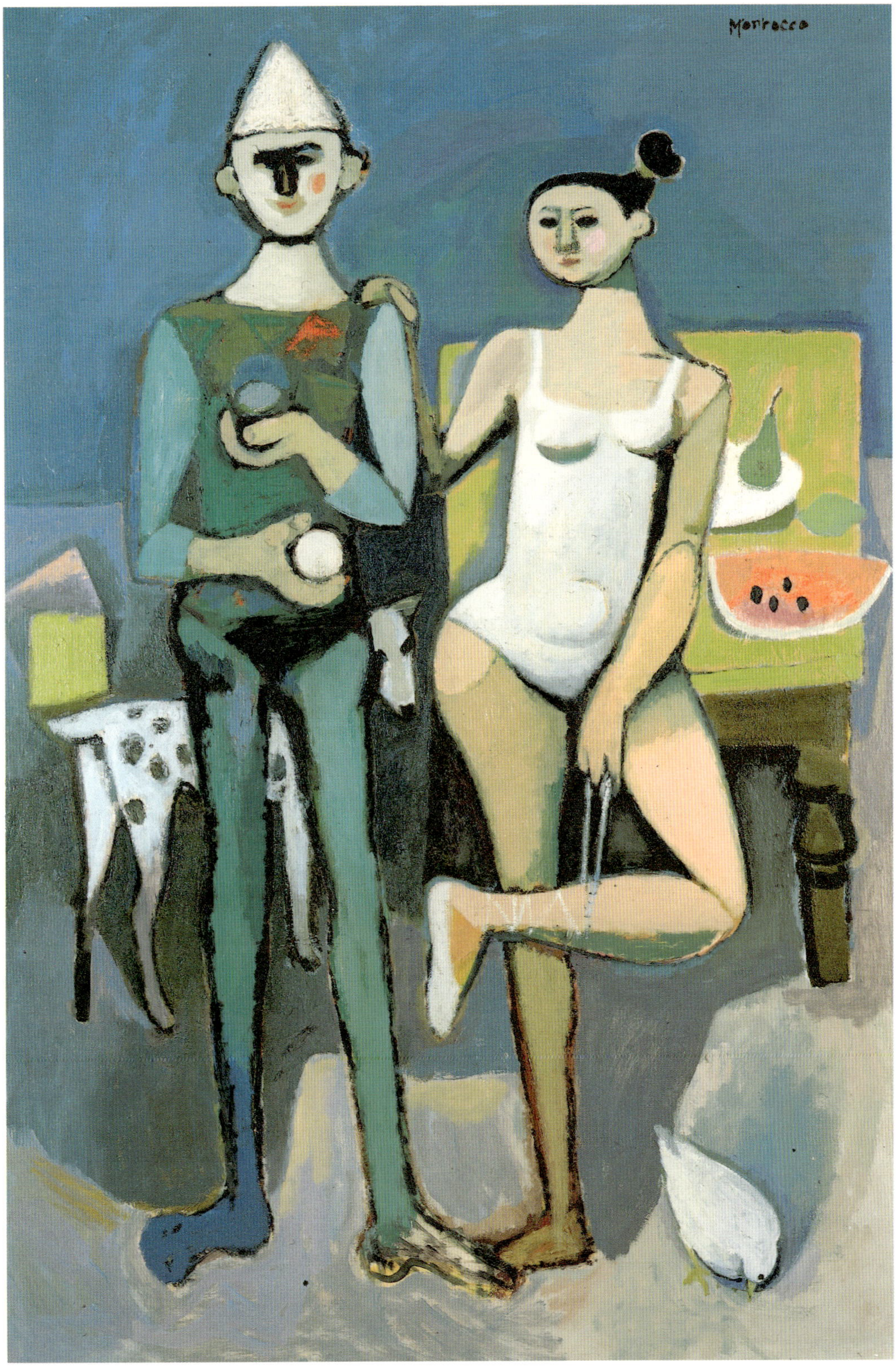

Plate 71 *Saltimbanchi*, c.1977 (Cat.115)

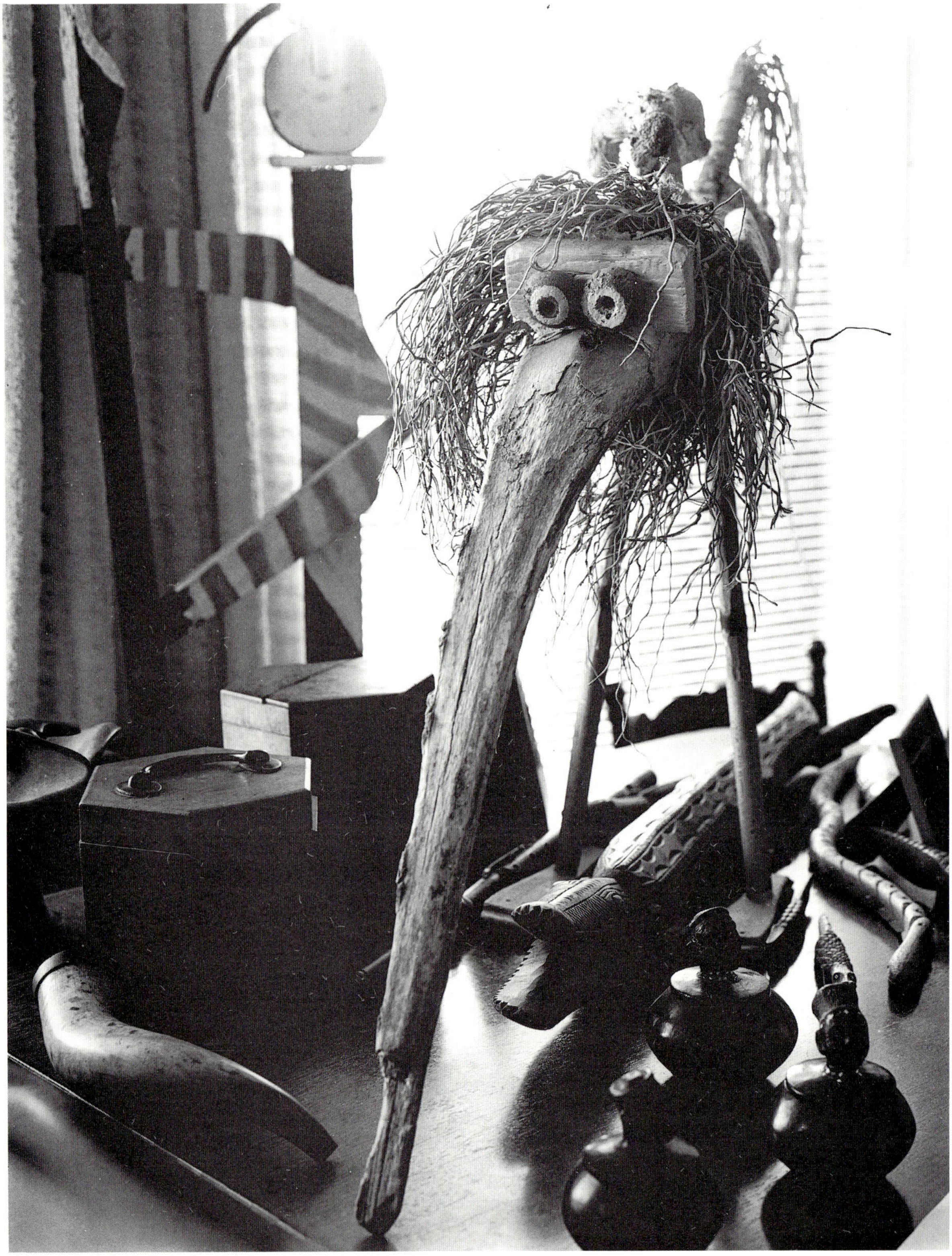

Plate 72 *Fantastic Bird*, junk sculpture from an Italian beach, 1960s

EXHIBITION CATALOGUE

Sizes are in both inches and centimetres, height before width.

1 **Self-portrait at 17 Years**
(Plate 6)
*c.*1935
oil on canvas
10 x 8 in. (25.4 x 20.3 cm.)
The Artist's Family

2 **Self-portrait** (Plate 2)
*c.*1935
pencil on paper
11½ x 9 in. (29.3 x 22.9 cm.)
The Artist's Family

3 **Male Model – Study**
(Plate 3)
*c.*1935
conté on paper
22 x 15 in. (55.9 x 38.1 cm.)
The Artist's Family

4 **Studies of Feet**
*c.*1935
conté on paper
9 x 6 in. (22.9 x 15.3 cm.)
& 6 x 9 in. (15.3 x 22.9 cm.)
The Artist's Family

5 **Still-life with Plaster Cast and Measuring Tape** (Plate 4)
*c.*1935
oil on canvas
24 x 19 in. (61 x 48.2 cm.)
The Artist's Family

6 **Girl in a Red Jersey**
*c.*1936 (with Robert Sivell)
oil on canvas
29 x 17 in. (73.7 x 43.2 cm.)
The Artist's Family

7 **Room to Let**
*c.*1945
linoprint on paper
14 x 9 in. (35.6 x 22.9 cm.)
The Artist's Family

8 **Self-portrait**
1943
oil on board
14 x 12 in. (35.6 x 30 cm.)
The Artist's Family

9 **Three Sailors on a Beach**
*c.*1946
oil on canvas
27½ x 30 in. (69.9 x 76.2 cm.)
The Artist's Family

10 **Brown Baby Laurie**
(Plate 5)
1947
oil on board
10½ x 8 in. (26.7 x 20.3 cm.)
The Artist's Family

11 **Vera** (Plate 8)
*c.*1947
pencil on paper
8¾ x 6¾ in. (22.3 x 17.2 cm.)
Mr and Mrs Val Morrocco

12 **Three Vesalius Figures for *Anatomy of the Human Body***
(Plate 9)
*c.*1948
ink on paper
each approx. 16 x 10½ in.
(40.5 x 16.5 cm.)
University of Aberdeen, Dept of Biomedical Sciences

13 **Winter in Holland Place**
(Plate 7)
1949
oil on board
12 x 15¼ in. (30.5 x 40 cm.)
The Artist's Family

14 **Nude Study – Vera** (Plate 12)
1949
conté on paper
17½ x 17½ in. (44.5 x 44.5 cm.)
The Artist's Family

15 **Holland Place, Sunday Evening (Vera and Celesta)**
(Plate 10)
*c.*1949/50
oil on board
16½ x 19 in. (41.9 x 48.3 cm.)
Mr and Mrs Val Morrocco

16 **Saturday Morning, Aberdeen**
1949 – *c.*1959
oil on canvas
22½ x 28 in. (57.2 x 71.1 cm.)
The Artist's Family

17 **Baking Cakes** (Plate 11)
1947-50
oil on canvas
32½ x 16½ in. (81.2 x 42 cm.)
Royal Scottish Academy

18 **Siesta**
*c.*1950
oil on board
12 x 15½ in. (30.5 x 39.4 cm.)
Eric and Patricia Auld

19 **Laurie with Red Shoes**
*c.*1950
oil on board
17½ x 13¾ in. (44.2 x 35.1 cm.)
The Artist's Family

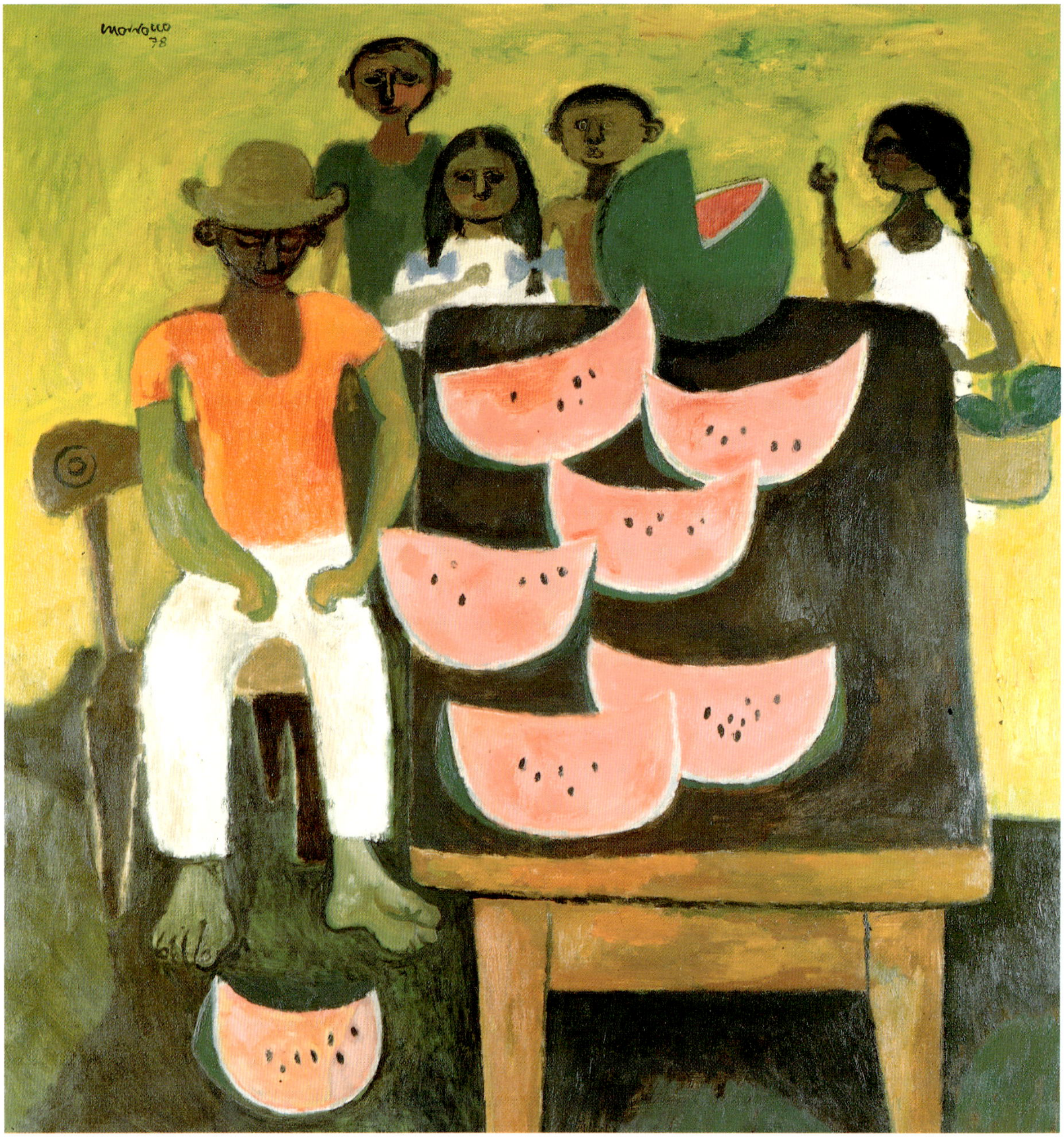

Plate 73 *Sleeping Melon Vendor*, 1978 (Cat.118)

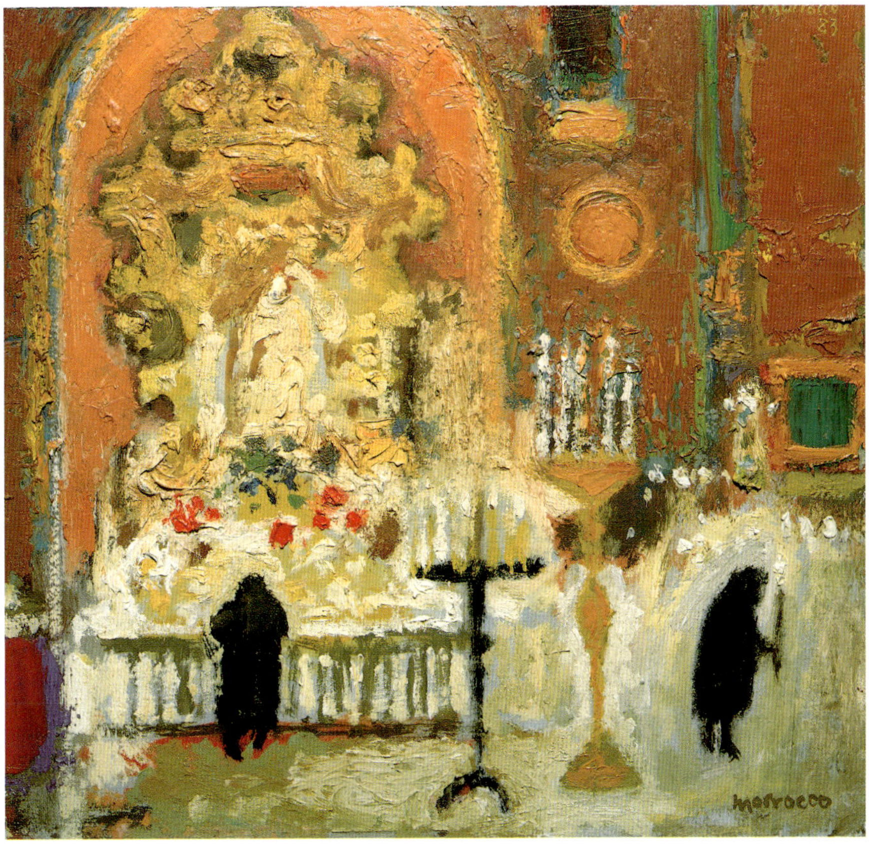

Plate 74 *Lighting Candles, San Marco*, 1983 (Cat.130)

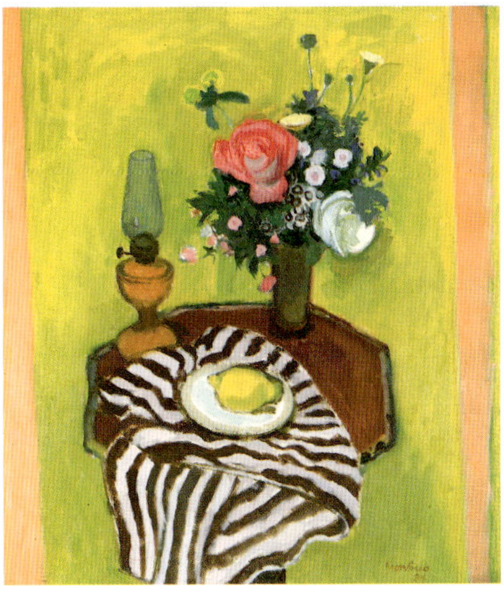

Plate 75 *Roses – Harmony in Yellow and Pink*, 1984 (Cat.133)

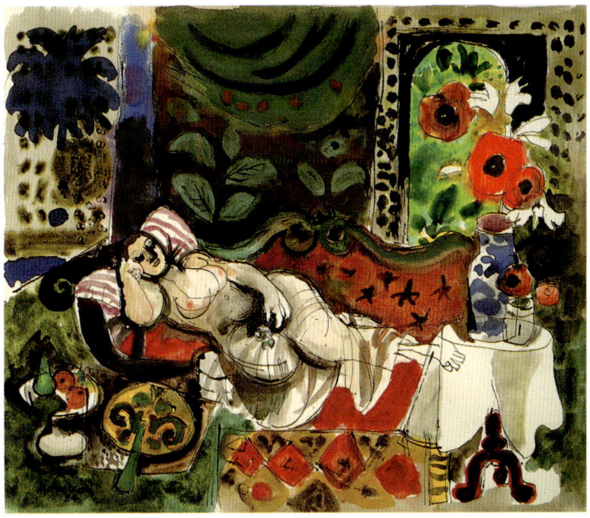

Plate 76 *Woman on a Divan*, 1984 (Cat.134)

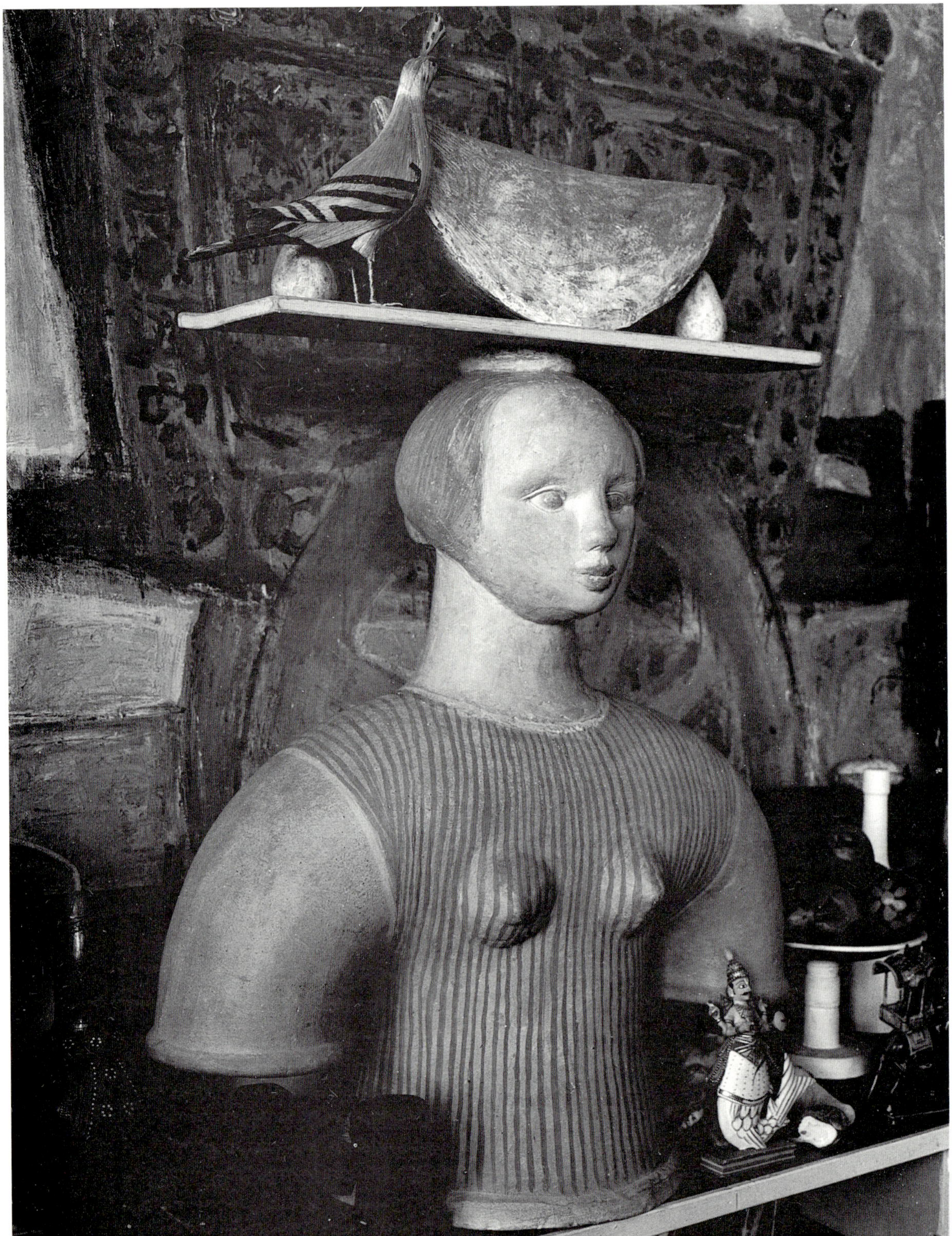

Plate 77 *Woman with Melon*, mixed media sculpture

20 **Nick at Three Months**
1950
oil on board
15 x 12½ in. (37.5 x 31.7 cm.)
Mr Nicholas Morrocco

21 **The Little Table**
*c.*1950
oil on canvas
27 x 29¾ in. (68 x 75cm.)
The Scottish Arts Council Collection

22 **The Artist's Mother**
1951
pastel on paper
24 x 29½ in. (61 x 75 cm.)
The Artist's Family

23 **A Winter Morning**
(Plate 13)
1951
oil on board
63 x 36 in. (159.7 x 91.5 cm.)
Aberdeen Art Gallery and Museums

24 **Self-portrait** (Plate 14)
*c.*1952
oil on canvas
31 x 24 in. (78.8 x 61 cm.)
The Artist's Family

25 **The Boys in the Kitchen**
(Plate 16)
*c.*1952
oil on canvas
36 x 26 in. (91.5 x 66 cm.)
The Artist's Family

26 **Profile in Grey (Vera)**
(Plate 15)
1952
oil on canvas
30 x 20½ in. (76.2 x 52.1 cm.)
The Artist's Family

27 **The Mantelpiece (Vera)**
(Plate 17)
1953
oil on canvas
18 x 24 in. (45.7 x 61 cm.)
The Artist's Family

28 **Castle at Rosas** (Plate 18)
1953
pen and wash on paper
15 x 22 in. (38.1 x 55.9 cm.)
The Artist's Family

29 **Breakfast**
*c.*1953
oil on canvas
29 x 23 in. (73.5 x 58.5 cm.)
Dumfriesshire Educational Trust Collection
(Gracefield Arts Centre)

30 **Hotel Marina, Rosas**
(Plate 21)
1953
oil on board
18½ x 25½ in. (47 x 65.8 cm.)
Private Collection

31 **Calle de Coscolano, Rosas**
*c.*1954
oil on board
24 x 30 in. (61 x 76.2 cm.)
City Art Centre, Edinburgh

32 **Sir John Ogilvy-Wedderburn Bt**
1954
oil on canvas
25 x 30 in. (63.5 x 76.2 cm.)
Lt Col Sir Andrew Ogilvy-Wedderburn Bt

33 **Laurie**
*c.*1954
oil on canvas
39 x 31 in. (99 x 78.8 cm.)
The Artist's Family

34 **Sun Worshippers**
(Plate 20)
1954
oil on canvas
59½ x 72 in. (151.2 x 182.9 cm.)
The Artist's Family

35 **Vera**
1954
pastel on paper
30 x 21 in. (76.2 x 53.4 cm.)
The Artist's Family

36 **Leon**
1954
pastel on paper
30 x 17 in. (76.2 x 43.2 cm.)
The Artist's Family

37 **Beatrice M. Rose**
(Headmistress of Aberdeen High School for Girls 1929-54)
1954
oil on canvas
36 x 28 in. (91.5 x 71.1 cm.)
Harlaw Academy (Aberdeen High School for Girls)

38 **The Blue Bedroom**
(Plate 19)
1954
oil on board
22 x 18¼ in. (56.1 x 46 cm.)
Glasgow Art Galleries and Museums

39 **Women of Anticoli**
*c.*1955
oil on board
19 x 23 in. (48.2 x 58.5 cm.)
Private Collection

40 **The Attic Bedroom**
(Plate 22)
1955
oil on canvas
52 x 32 in. (132.1 x 81.3 cm.)
Dundee Art Galleries and Museums

41 **Festa di Sant' Anna**
1956
indian ink and watercolour on paper
18½ x 15½ in. (47 x 39.4 cm)
Mrs I. Barnet

42 **Girl with Laundry**
*c.*1956
gouache on paper
22 x 20 in. (55.9 x 50.8 cm)
Private Collection

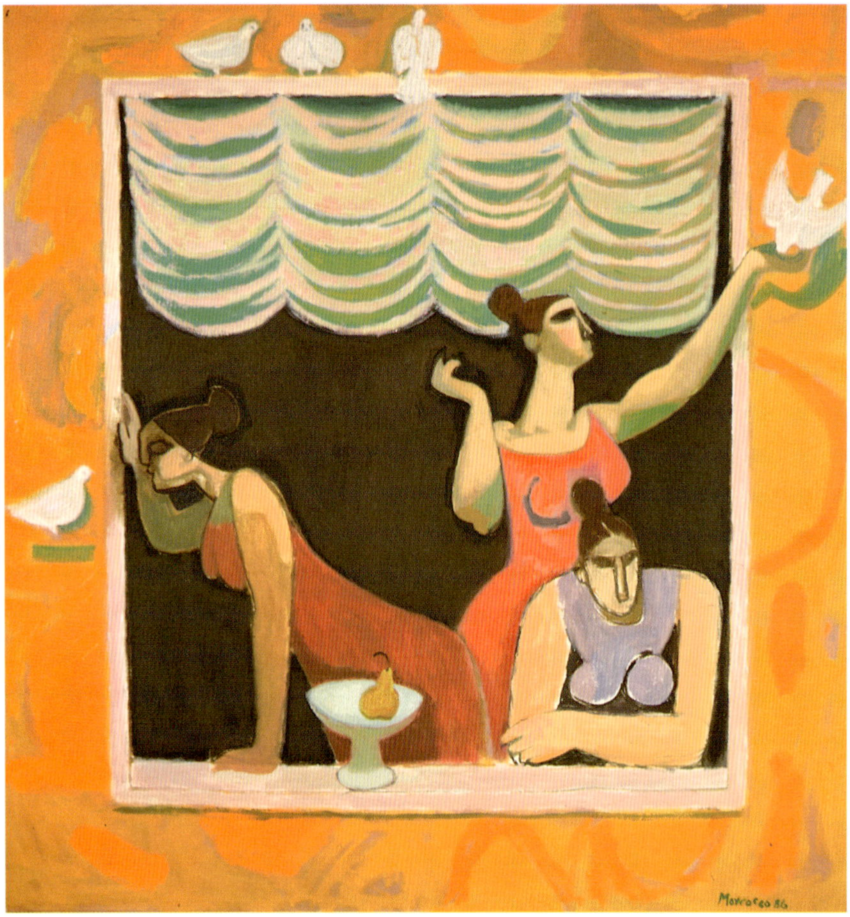

Plate 78 *Three Sisters of Lucca,* 1986 (Cat.141)

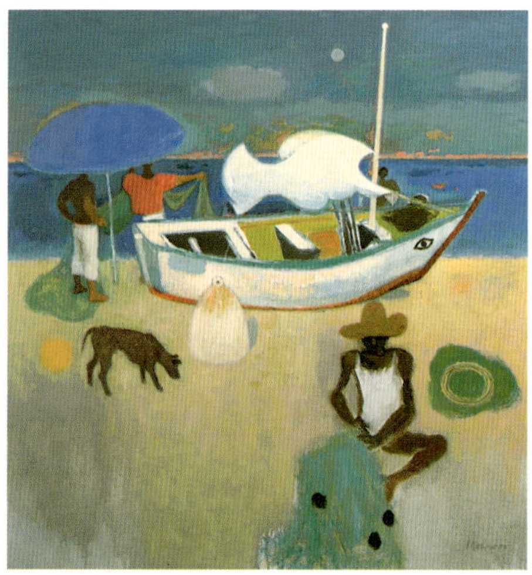

Plate 79 *Afternoon at Fondachello,* 1985 (Cat.138)

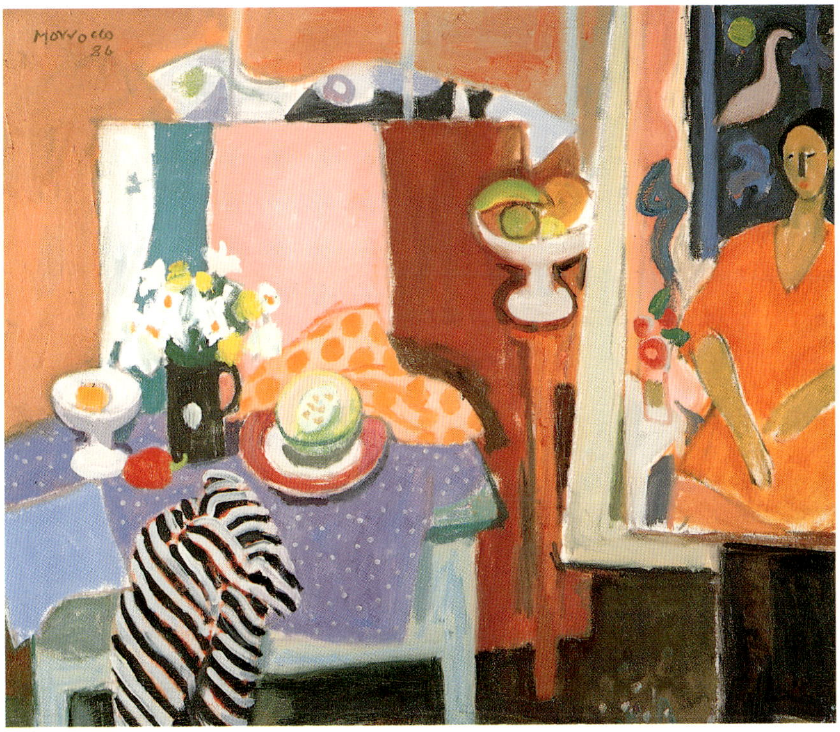

Plate 80 *The Studio*, 1986 (Cat.139)

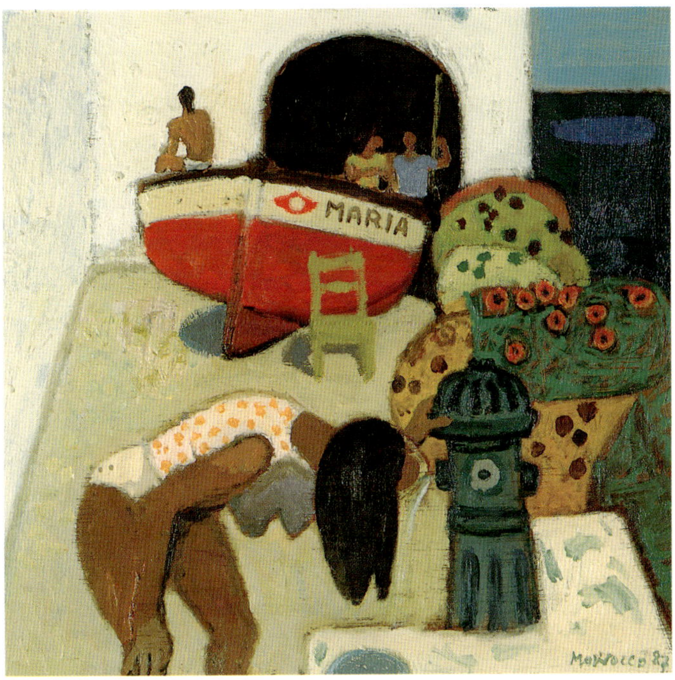

Plate 81 *Maria*, 1987 (Cat.146)

43 **I Poveri**
*c.*1957
oil on board
7 x 11½ in. (17.8 x 29.2 cm.)
Private Collection

44 **Rocky Path, Anticoli**
*c.*1957
oil on board
20 x 28 in. (50.8 x 71.1 cm.)
Private Collection

45 **Anticoli** (Plate 28)
1958
oil on canvas
24 x 20 in. (61 x 50.8 cm.)
Private Collection

46 **Interior with a Hungry Cat**
(Plate 26)
*c.*1958
oil on canvas
79 x 49 in. (200.8 x 124.5 cm.)
The Artist's Family

47 **The Second Chef**
1958
oil on canvas
50 x 30 in. (127 x 76.2 cm.)
The Artist's Family

48 **I Poveri** (Plate 27)
*c.*1959
oil on canvas
40 x 60 in. (101.6 x 152.4 cm.)
The Artist's Family

49 **Sicilian Women**
*c.*1959
oil on board
20½ x 14½ in. (52 x 37 cm.)
Private Collection

50 **Riders on a Beach**
(Plate 30)
1959
oil on board
47¼ x 57¼ in. (120.5 x 145 cm.)
The Scottish Arts Council
Collection

51 **The Chinese Teapot**
(Plate 32)
*c.*1959
oil on board
15½ x 11½ in. (39.5 x 29.2 cm.)
The Artist's Family

52 **Sicilian Cart** (Plate 31)
*c.*1960
oil on canvas
21 x 34 in. (53.3 x 86.4 cm.)
Private Collection

53 **Vera with Sunhat**
*c.*1960
conté on paper
17 x 11½ in. (43.2 x 29.2 cm.)
The Artist's Family

54 **Peasant Ploughing**
*c.*1960/62
gouache on paper
18½ x 26 in. (47 x 66 cm.)
Private Collection

55 **Ave Maria** (Plate 33)
*c.*1960
oil on canvas
40 x 30 in. (101.6 x 76.2 cm.)
The Artist's Family

56 **Red Hill, Anticoli I**
(Plate 34)
*c.*1960
oil on canvas
34½ x 60 in. (88 x 152.5 cm.)
McLean Museum and Art
Gallery, Greenock

57 **Laurie Morrocco**
1961
oil on canvas
39 x 31 in. (99 x 78.8 cm.)
The Artist's Family

58 **View of Anticoli Corrado**
*c.*1962
watercolour on paper
28 x 20½ in. (71.2 x 52.1 cm.)
The Artist's Family

59 **Confession** (Plate 35)
*c.*1962
oil on board
60 x 41 in. (152.5 x 104 cm.)
The Artist's Family

60 **Ave Maria**
*c.*1962
watercolour on paper
31 x 26½ in. (78.8 x 67.3 cm.)
The Artist's Family

61 **Cartoon for Mural,
St Columba's, Glenrothes**
*c.*1962
tempera and gouache on paper
12½ x 72½ in. (31.8 x 184.2 cm.)
Private Collection

62 **Professor John Walton**
1962
oil on canvas
42 x 39 in. (106.6 x 99 cm.)
Hunterian Art Gallery,
University of Glasgow

63 **Setting Sun II** (Plate 39)
*c.*1962
oil on canvas
41 x 38 in. (104 x 96 cm.)
The Scottish Arts Council
Collection

64 **Red Hill, Anticoli II**
(Plate 37)
*c.*1962
oil on canvas
48 x 42½ in. (121.9 x 108 cm.)
Low and Bonar PLC, Dundee

65 **Blind Fortune-teller**
(Plate 38)
*c.*1962
oil on board
36 x 30 in. (91.5 x 76.2 cm.)
The Artist's Family

66 **Boy with Bowl of Eggs**
(Plate 43)
*c.*1962
oil on canvas
26 x 18 in. (66 x 45.8 cm.)
The Royal Bank of Scotland plc

67 **Hill Village and Monastery**
(Plate 42)
*c.*1963
oil on canvas
40 x 30 in. (101.6 x 76.2 cm.)
The Artist's Family

68 **Joseph H. Wright**
(Past President of Royal College of Physicians
and Surgeons of Glasgow)
(Plate 41)
*c.*1962
oil on canvas
44 x 36 in. (111.8 x 91.5 cm.)
Royal College of Physicians and Surgeons of Glasgow

69 **Anna Lisa**
*c.*1964
oil on canvas
41 x 34 in. (104.2 x 86.4 cm.)
The Artist's Family

70 **Hill Village and Road**
*c.*1964
oil on canvas
25 x 30 in. (63.5 x 76.2 cm.)
The Artist's Family

71 **The Rt Hon Lord Boyd Orr of Brechin**
(Chancellor of Glasgow University) (Plate 48)
1964
pastel on paper
17 x 13 in. (43.2 x 33 cm.)
Hunterian Art Gallery, University of Glasgow

72 **Methven**
1965
oil on canvas
40 x 32 in. (101.6 x 81.3 cm.)
National Galleries of Scotland

73 **Door in Orbitello**
(Plate 45)
1966
mixed media construction
71 x 53 in. (180.3 x 134.7 cm.)
The Artist's Family

74 **Girl with Melons**
(Plate 47)
1966
watercolour on paper
29½ x 20 in. (75 x 50.8 cm.)
Mrs Joyce H. Clark

75 **Study for Liff Hospital Mural**
1966
watercolour and pencil on paper
6½ x 16 in. (16.5 x 40.7 cm.)
Private Collection

76 **Watering the Donkeys, Cefalu** (Plate 46)
1966
pen and ink and watercolour on paper
26¼ x 32¼ in. (66.9 x 82.2 cm.)
Aberdeen Art Gallery and Museums

77 **Melon Seller**
1967
oil on board
12 x 10¼ in. (30.5 x 26 cm.)
Private Collection

78 **Dave Phillips**
1968
oil on canvas
19 x 15½ in. (48.3 x 39.5 cm.)
The Artist's Family

79 **Self-portrait with Wife and Child and Conde, Duque de Olivares** (Platc 52)
*c.*1968
oil on canvas
70 x 98 in. (177.8 x 249 cm.)
The Artist's Family

80 **Sunflowers** (Plate 51)
1969
ink, wash and charcoal on paper
24½ x 40½ in.
(62.2 x 102.9 cm.)
Private Collection

81 **Riders in an Estuary**
1969
watercolour on paper
26 x 35 in. (66 x 88.9 cm.)
Professor R. A. Kennedy

82 **The Key (Mariage de Convenance)** (Plate 54)
1969
oil on board
33 x 48 in. (83.9 x 122 cm.)
The Artist's Family

83 **Sacred and Profane**
1969
oil on board
40 x 50 in. (101.6 x 127 cm.)
The Artist's Family

84 **Dirigible over Deauville**
(Plate 55)
1969
oil on canvas
40 x 50 in. (101.6 x 127 cm.)
The Artist's Family

85 **Self-portrait in Mexican Hat (The Studio)**
*c.*1970
oil on board
19 x 24 in. (48.2 x 61 cm.)
J. McIntosh Patrick

86 **Making Conserva**
*c.*1970
oil on board
9 x 9 in. (22.9 x 22.9 cm.)
Alex McCallum and Colin Brown

87 **The Beach at Stromboli**
(Plate 53)
*c.*1970
oil on board
44 x 55 in. (111.7 x 139.7 cm.)
The Artist's Family

88 **Portrait of Vera** (Plate 58)
1971
oil on canvas
54 x 34 in. (137.2 x 86.4 cm.)
The Artist's Family

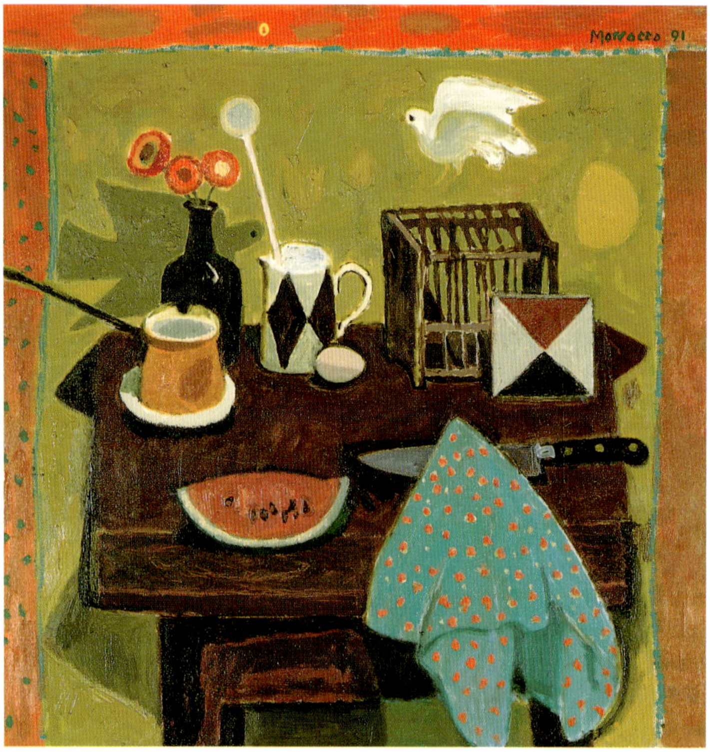

Plate 82 *Homage à Braque*, 1991 (Cat.151)

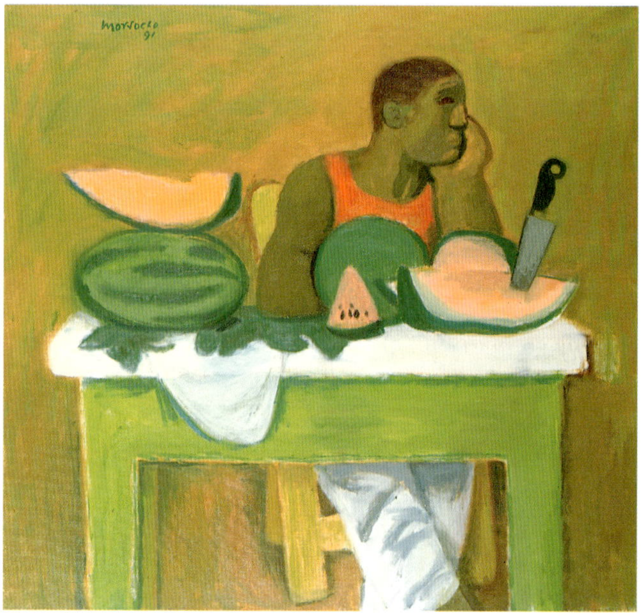

Plate 83 *Man with Watermelons*, 1991 (Cat.152)

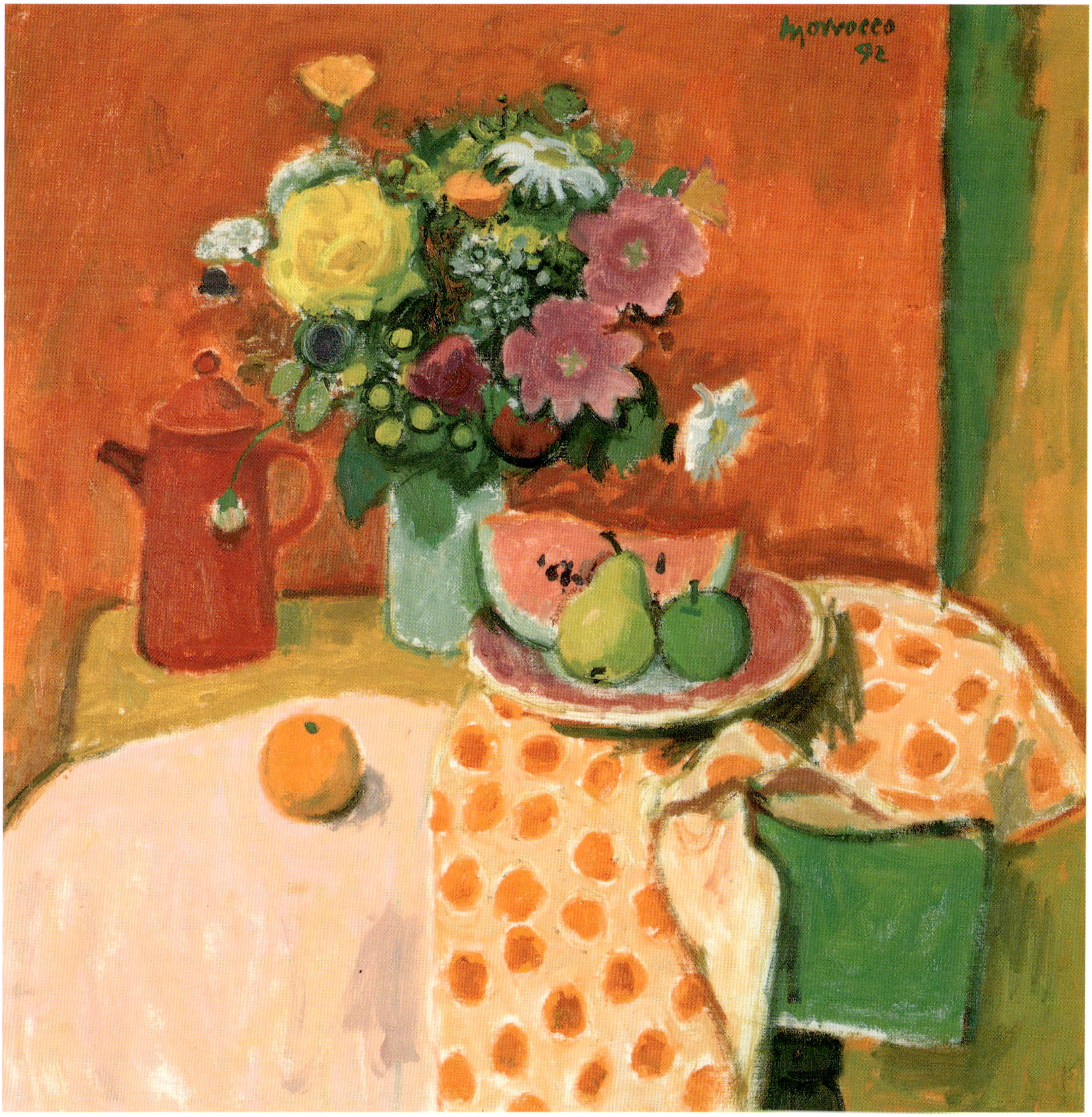

Plate 84 *Fruit and Flowers on a Red Ground*, 1992 (Cat.153)

89 **Girl with Laundry**
(Plate 60)
1971
oil on canvas
33 x 24 in. (83.8 x 61 cm.)
Private Collection

90 **Siesta** (Plate 59)
*c.*1971
oil on canvas
60 x 63 in. (152.5 x 160 cm.)
The Artist's Family

91 **Lisa on Hobbyhorse**
(Plate 57)
1971
conté and charcoal on paper
21½ x 19 in. (54.6 x 48.2 cm.)
The Artist's Family

92 **Yehudi Menuhin at the Caird Hall** (Plate 64)
1972
oil on board
62 x 50 in. (157.5 x 127 cm.)
The Artist's Family

93 **Dull Day at the Lido**
(Plate 49)
1972
size tempera on canvas
70 x 70 in. (177.8 x 177.8 cm.)
The Artist's Family

94 **Fine Day at the Lido**
(Plate 50)
1972
size tempera on canvas
70 x 70 in. (177.8 x 177.8 cm.)
The Artist's Family

95 **The Steps to the Roof**
1972
oil on board
18 x 11 in. (45.7 x 28 cm.)
Private Collection

96 **Bird Seller**
1973
oil on board
11 x 18 in. (28 x 20.3 cm.)
Victor Young

97 **Spaghetti Eater**
1973
oil on board
11 x 9 in (28 x 22.9 cm.)
Mr and Mrs Scott Christie

98 **Fields Above Gourdon**
1973
oil on board
9 x 10 in. (22.9 x 25.4 cm.)
Private Collection

99 **Fondamenta Pescheria, Burano** (Plate 63)
1973
watercolour sketch on paper
10¾ x 10½ in. (27.3 x 26.7 cm.)
The Artist's Family

100 **Santa Maria della Salute from Ponte della Pagia**
1973
watercolour sketch on paper
10¾ x 10½ in. (27.3 x 26.7 cm.)
The Artist's Family

101 **Campo Santi Giovanni e Paulo**
1974
oil on canvas
36 x 36 in. (91.5 x 91.5 cm.)
Private Collection

102 **Girl on a Balcony**
1974
oil on canvas
30 x 28 in. (76.2 x 71.1 cm.)
Private Collection

103 **Three Hens**
*c.*1974
oil on board
14 x 11 in. (35.5 x 28 cm.)
Lillie Art Gallery, Milngavie

104 **Still-life with Fruit and Egg**
(Plate 67)
*c.*1974
oil on board
24 x 30 in. (61 x 76.2 cm.)
The Artist's Family

105 **The Honourable Lord Cameron** (Plate 65)
1974
oil on canvas
50 x 48 in. (127 x 121.9 cm.)
Talbot Rice Gallery, University of Edinburgh

106 **Evening at Cefalu**
1975
oil on canvas
50 x 66 in. (127 x 167.7 cm.)
The Artist's Family

107 **Grande Natura Morta Napolitana** (Plate 66)
1975
oil on board
59 x 59 in. (150 x 150 cm.)
The Artist's Family

108 **Documentary Self-portrait**
(Plate 68)
1975
oil on board
four panels, overall 59 x 49 in.
(149.9 x 124.5 cm.)
The Artist's Family

109 **Piazza San Marco in Flood**
1976
oil on board
18 x 24 in. (45.7 x 61 cm.)
Mr and Mrs Larry Rolland

110 **Turcomania** (Plate 70)
1976
oil on canvas
42 x 38 in. (106.7 x 96 cm.)
Robert Fleming Holdings Limited

111 **Harlequin**
1977
oil on board
11¼ x 8¼ in. (28.6 x 21 cm.)
Mrs Joyce H. Clark

112 **Tay Bridge, Winter**
1977
oil on card
30¼ x 40¼ in. (76.9 x 102.2 cm.)
Robert Fleming Holdings Limited

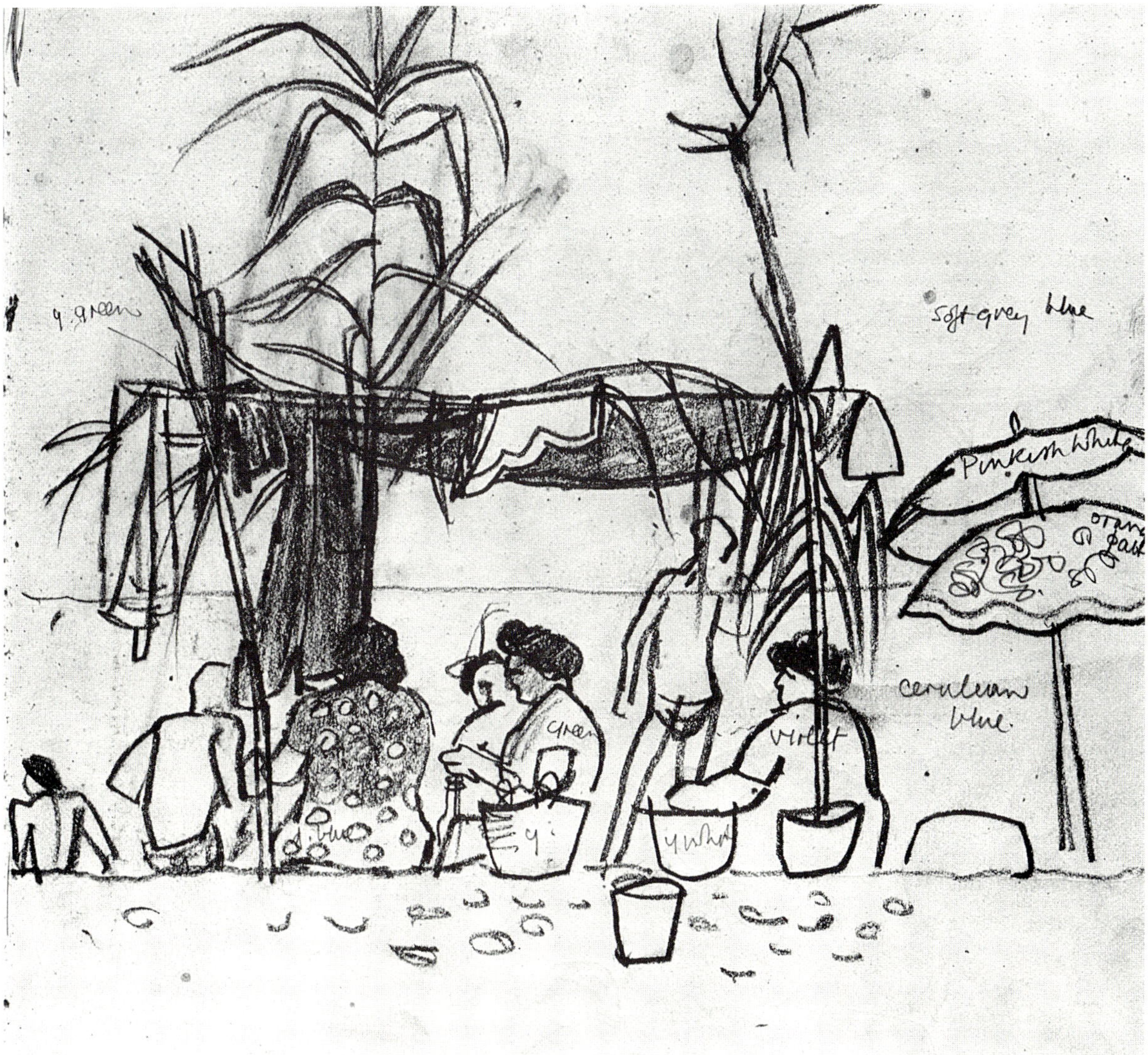

Plate 85 Original sketch for *Peasants on a Beach*, 1970s

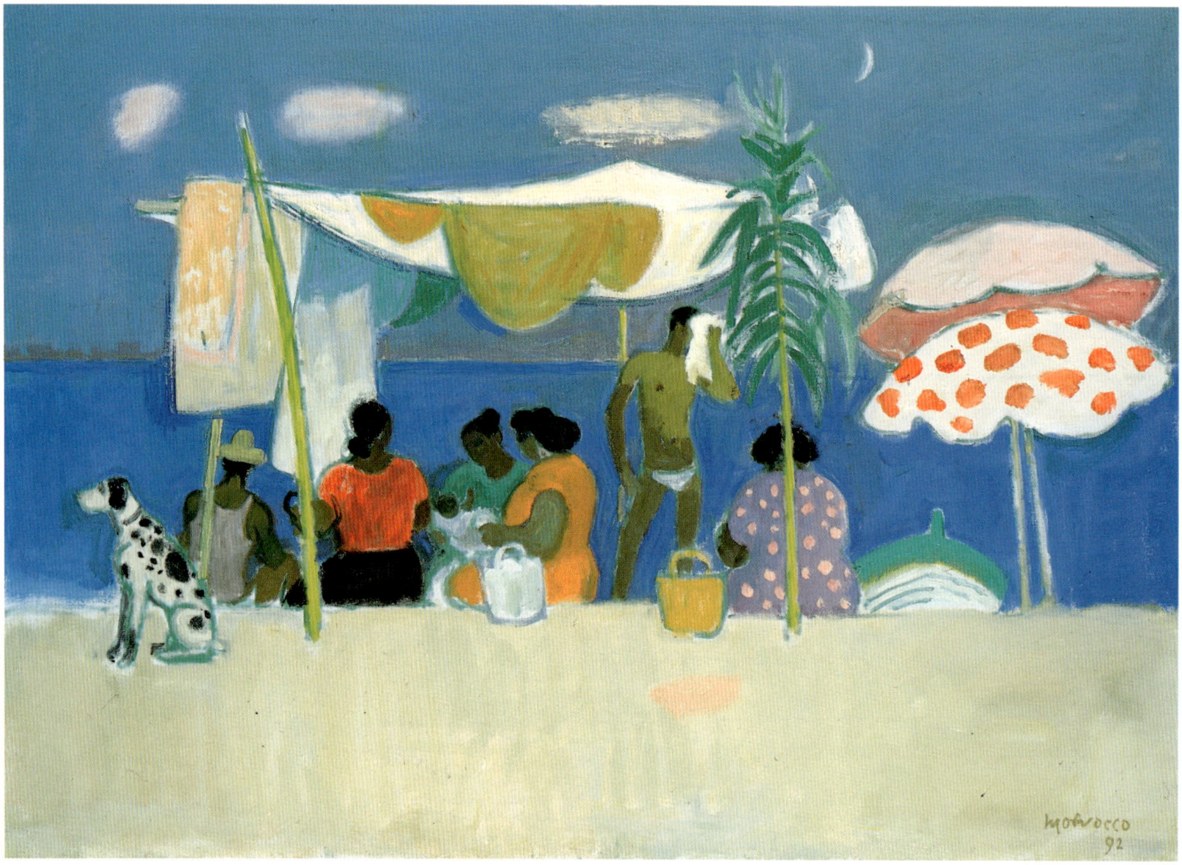

Plate 86 *Peasants on a Beach*, 1992 (Cat.154)

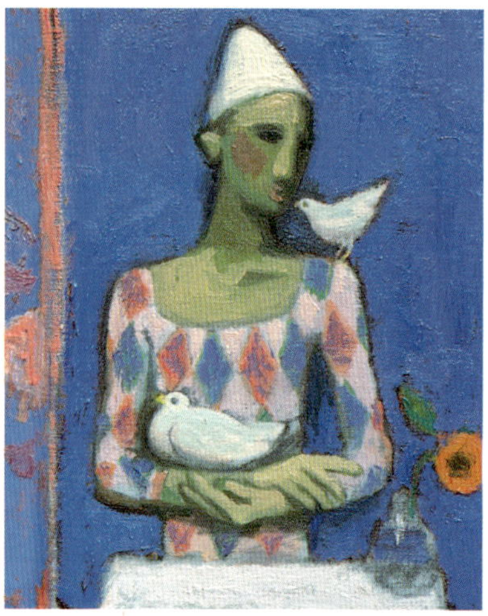

Plate 87 *Clown with Doves*, 1992 (Cat.155)

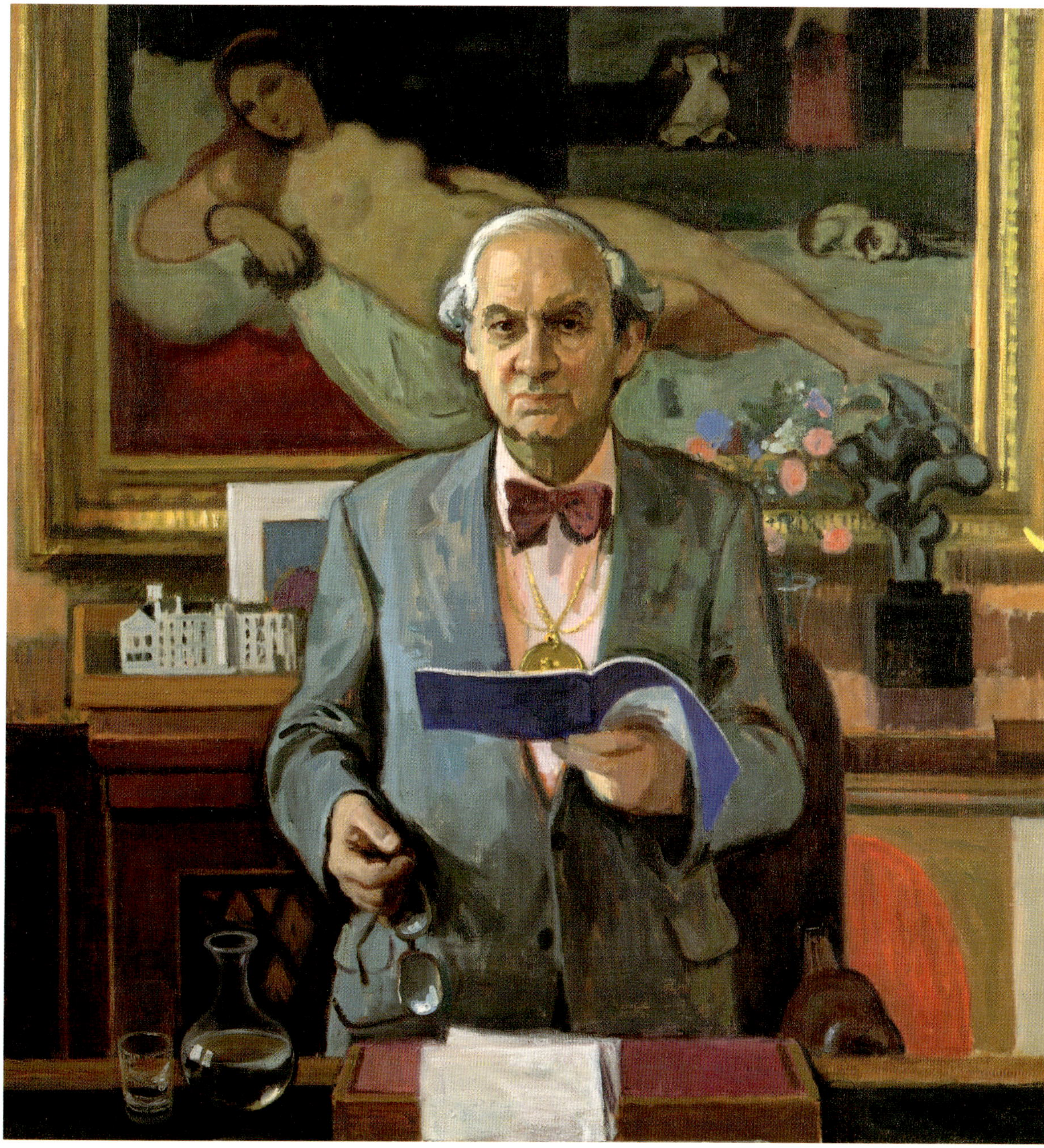

Plate 88 *Sir Anthony Wheeler*, 1992 (Cat.157)

113 **Still-life with Horse and Cart**
1977
oil on canvas
36 x 24 in. (91.5 x 61 cm.)
Private Collection

114 **Ca d'Oro, Venice**
1977
watercolour on paper
25 x 27 in. (63 x 68 cm.)
Private Collection

115 **Saltimbanchi** (Plate 71)
*c.*1977
oil on board
60 x 41 in. (152.5 x 104.2 cm.)
The Artist's Family

116 **Pit Orchestra**
1978
oil on board
43¼ x 48 in. (110 x 121 cm.)
Lillie Art Gallery, Milngavie

117 **Woman at a Window**
1978
oil on board
5½ x 7½ in. (14 x 19 cm.)
P. B. Findlay

118 **Sleeping Melon Vendor** (Plate 73)
1978
oil on canvas
53½ x 52 in. (135.9 x 132.1 cm.)
Private Collection

119 **Breakfast**
1978
oil on canvas
36 x 36 in. (91.5 x 91.5 cm.)
The University of St Andrews, Fine Art Department

120 **Wilbur Muirhead** (Captain of the Royal and Ancient Golf Club 1977-78)
1978
portrait study
pastel on paper
14 x 11 in. (35.6 x 27.9 cm.)
The Artist's Family

121 **Majorcan Interior**
1979
oil on board
16½ x 14 in. (41.9 x 35.6 cm.)
Ronald Craig

122 **Peasant Women by the Sea**
1979
oil on canvas
9½ x 13 in. (24 x 33 cm.)
Mr and Mrs Glen L. Pride

123 **View of Ronda**
*c.*1980
oil on board
11 x 13 in. (28 x 33 cm.)
Beryl Kidd

124 **Professor James Drever** (Principal of Dundee University 1966-78)
*c.*1980
portrait study
pastel on paper
18 x 15 in. (45.8 x 38.1 cm.)
The Artist's Family

125 **Still-life with Blue Bird, Evening**
1981
oil on board
25 x 30 in. (63.5 x 76.2 cm.)
Priscilla Anderson, Thackeray Gallery

126 **Caged Birds at Night** (Plate 62)
1981
indian ink on paper
29½ x 21½ in. (75 x 54.5 cm.)
The Scottish Arts Council Collection

127 **Women by the Sea** (Plate 69)
1981
oil on canvas
50 x 41 in. (127 x 104 cm.)
The Artist's Family

128 **Still-life with Pears, Pomegranate and Melon**
1981
oil on canvas
42 x 38 in. (106.7 x 96.5 cm.)
Grampian Television PLC

129 **Mr Tahir in Ward 15**
*c.*1982
triptych, oil on canvas, overall 24 x 78 in. (61 x 198.2 cm.)
The Artist's Family

130 **Lighting Candles, San Marco** (Plate 74)
1983
oil on board
13 x 14 in. (33 x 35.5 cm.)
Private Collection

131 **Sunflowers on a Blue Ground**
1983
oil on canvas
47½ x 29½ in. (120.6 x 74.9 cm.)
Robert Fleming Holdings Limited

132 **Picnic on the Beach**
1983
oil on canvas
23 x 33 in. (58.5 x 83.9 cm.)
Mr and Mrs Robert Steedman

133 **Roses – Harmony in Yellow and Pink** (Plate 75)
1984
oil on canvas
36 x 32 in. (91.5 x 81.3 cm.)
Mr and Mrs Larry Rolland

134 **Woman on a Divan** (Plate 76)
1984
gouache on paper
25 x 30 in. (63.5 x 76.2 cm.)
Private Collection

135 **The Lord Clydesmuir KT**
*c.*1985
portrait study
pastel on paper
24 x 19 in. (61 x 48.3 cm.)
The Artist's Family

136 **Still-life on a Red Ground**
1985
oil on canvas
31 x 34 in. (78.8 x 86.4 cm.)
Priscilla Anderson, Thackeray Gallery

137 **Burano**
1985
oil on board
22 x 24 in. (55.9 x 61 cm.)
Alex McCallum and Colin Brown

138 **Afternoon at Fondachello**
(Plate 79)
1985
oil on canvas
51 x 48 in. (129.5 x 121.9 cm.)
The Artist's Family

139 **The Studio** (Plate 80)
1986
oil on canvas
30 x 36 in. (76.2 x 91.5 cm.)
Private Collection

140 **Still-life on Red Cloth**
(Plate 1)
1986
oil on canvas
39 x 45 in. (99 x 114.5 cm.)
Dundee Art Galleries and Museums

141 **Three Sisters of Lucca**
(Plate 78)
1986
oil on canvas
50 x 48 in. (127 x 122 cm.)
Collection of Dundas and Wilson

142 **Nude Woman with Cat**
1986
oil on canvas
24 x 19 in. (61 x 48.3 cm.)
Alex McCallum and Colin Brown

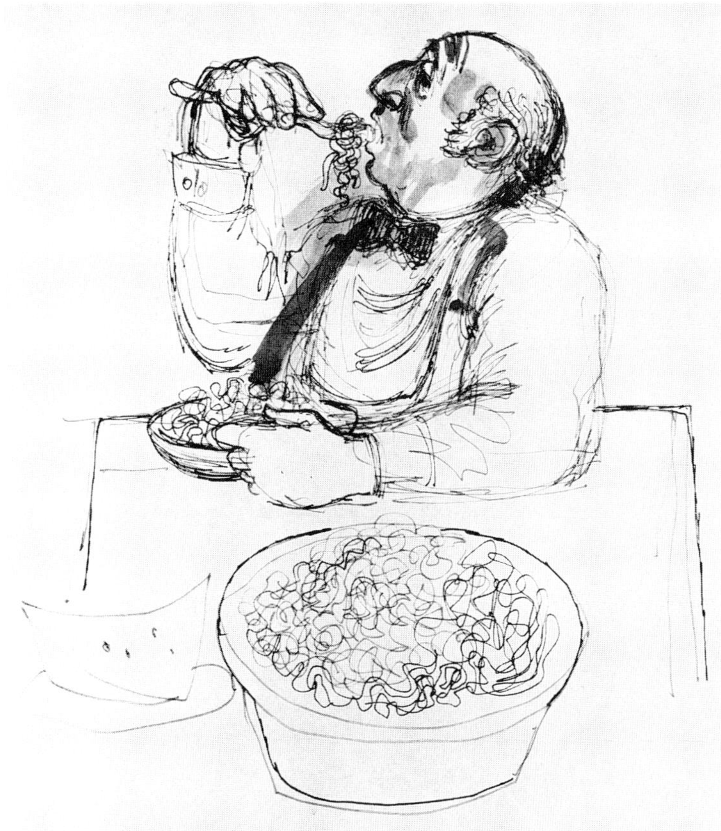

Plate 89 *Eating Spaghetti – Self-portrait* (page from sketchbook)

143 **Winter Moon**
1986
oil on canvas
30 x 28 in. (76.2 x 71.1 cm.)
Private Collection

144 **Vera at her Dressing Table**
1987
oil on canvas
24 x 24 in. (61 x 61 cm.)
Private Collection

145 **The Spaghetti Eater**
1987
oil on board
5½ x 7½ in. (14 x 19 cm.)
Private Collection

146 **Maria** (Plate 81)
1987
oil on canvas
15 x 16 in. (38.1 x 40 cm.)
Private Collection

147 **Siesta in the Abruzzi**
1988
oil on board
23 x 21 in. (58.5 x 53.4 cm.)
Mr and Mrs Ray Treen

148 **Siesta on the Lido**
1988
oil on board
21½ x 26½ in. (54.6 x 67.3 cm.)
Alex McCallum and Colin Brown

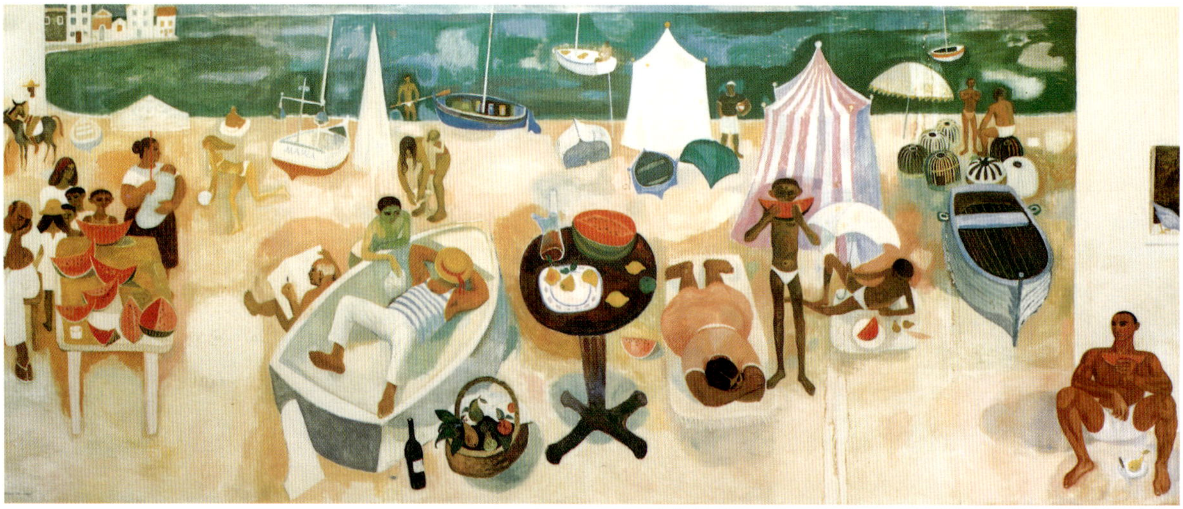

Plate 90 *Liff Hospital Mural*, 1966, tempera, 120 x 300 in.

149 **Still-life with Compote of Green Pears**
1989
oil on canvas
28 x 30 in. (71 x 76 cm.)
Mr and Mrs Andrew Merrylees

150 **Ricordo di Sicilia**
1989
triptych, oil on canvas
39 x 70 in. (99 x 177.7 cm.)
The Artist's Family

151 **Homage à Braque**
(Plate 82)
1991
oil on canvas
30 x 30 in. (76.2 x 76.2 cm.)
Private Collection

152 **Man with Watermelons**
(Plate 83)
1991
oil on canvas
28 x 30 in (71.1 x 76.2 cm.)
Private Collection

153 **Fruit and Flowers on a Red Ground** (Plate 84)
1992
oil on canvas
28 x 28 in. (71.1 x 71.1 cm.)
Private Collection

154 **Peasants on a Beach** (Plate 86)
1992
oil on canvas
30 x 42 in. (76.2 x 106.7 cm.)
Private Collection

155 **Clown with Doves**
(Plate 87)
1992
oil on board
10 x 9 in. (25.4 x 22.9 cm.)
Dr P. Gould

156 **Woman with Watermelon**
1992
oil on board
10 x 10 in. (25.4 x 25.4 cm.)
Private Collection

157 **Sir Anthony Wheeler**
(President of the Royal Scottish Academy 1983-90)
(Plate 88)
1992
oil on canvas
48 x 45¼ in. (122 x 115 cm.)
Royal Scottish Academy